A FRIENDLY GUIDE TO VATICAN II

MAX VODOLA

Contents

Title page:
Celebrations in Rome at the canonisation of Pope John XXIII

Opposite page: Pope John XXIII when he was Monsignor Roncalli, Bulgaria in 1925

Chapter 1

Historical Background

Councils in the Church

A council is an occasional gathering of church representatives, mainly bishops, for the purpose of consultation and decision-making on important matters in the life of the Church. The Catholic Church teaches that such councils are convoked under the inspiration of the Holy Spirit in order to determine issues relating to doctrine, discipline and theological practice binding on all believers. The form, style, length and structure of councils have varied greatly over the centuries, often in relation to disputed theological issues that give rise to the councils within the historical context of the time.

Vatican II or the Second Vatican Council (1962-65) is designated the Twenty-First Ecumenical Council, the first being Nicaea in 325. The early councils concentrated largely on the 'Christological' controversies, clarifying in a theological way the unity of Christ's human and divine natures. The Creed that is recited at Mass on Sundays was formulated and refined in the course of these early councils. A close study of councils also reveals often fiery and lengthy debate over controversial and contentious issues. History also teaches us that councils often arouse great interest and expectations.

Below: Statue of Pope Pius IX in Basilica Santa Maria Maggiore, Rome

Did you know?

There have been twenty-one Ecumenical Councils in the history of the Church

Council	Date
1. Nicaea I	325
2. Constantinople I	381
3. Ephesus	431
4. Chalcedon	451
5. Constantinople II	553
6. Constantinople III	680
7. Nicaea II	787
8. Constantinople IV	869
9. Lateran I	1123
10. Lateran II	1139
11. Lateran III	1179
12. Lateran IV	1215
13. Lyons I	1245
14. Lyons II	1274
15. Vienne	1311
16. Constance	1414–18
17. Florence (also known as Basel-Ferrara-Florence-Rome)	1431–45
18. Lateran V	1512–17
19. Trent	1545–63
20. Vatican I	1869–70
21. Vatican II	1962–65

Pope John XXIII—Early Years

Angelo Giuseppe Roncalli was born on 25 November 1881 in the small village of Sotto il Monte in Bergamo, northern Italy. He was the fourth of eleven children and the first son to his parents, local tenant farmers. By all accounts, the young Angelo had an unremarkable upbringing. Later, as pope, Roncalli would recall with affection the relative poverty and simplicity of his early years. His primary education was in the local village school. Later, expressing a desire for the priesthood, Angelo was sent to the minor seminary in Bergamo followed by studies in Rome.

As a teenage seminarian, Roncalli commenced what would become his great spiritual testament, *Journal of a Soul*, and he remained faithful in maintaining this journal throughout his life, including during his relatively short papacy. Much in the journal is consistent with the images of him as pope – kind, benign, humble, open-hearted and eager to do the will of God by following the example of the saints. On the surface, *Journal of a Soul* reflects the spirituality of the time through a young aspirant to the priesthood. Delving deeper, it details Roncalli's resolutions regarding prayer and fasting, going to confession, praying the rosary, visits to the Blessed Sacrament, and examination of conscience. However, the journal also reflects the intersection in Roncalli between spiritual development and intellectual formation, his capacity to reflect on his experience in the light of Christian history and his ability to situate himself within the context of some of the burning theological questions of the day.

Roncalli arrived in Rome early in 1901 to complete his studies for the priesthood. There was great intellectual and theological ferment in Rome regarding the use of the 'historical-critical' method of biblical studies which was used widely in Protestant circles but frowned upon by Catholic authorities. Roncalli was surrounded by professors and fellow students who wanted the Catholic Church to embrace with vigour this critical study of theology and the bible. The

Below: Birthplace of Pope John XXIII, Sotto il Monte, Bergamo, Italy

'would-be' historian expressed some cautious openness to these ideas and entries in *Journal of a Soul* reveal moments of deep spiritual and intellectual struggle:

> It will always be my principle, in all spheres of religious knowledge and in all theological and biblical questions, to find out first of all the traditional teaching of the Church, and on this basis to judge the findings of contemporary scholarship. I do not despise criticism and I shall be most careful not to think ill of critics or to treat them with disrespect. On the contrary, I love it. I shall be glad to keep up with the most recent findings, I shall study the new systems of thought and their continual evolution and their trends; criticism for me is light, is truth, and there is only one truth, which is sacred (A.G. Roncalli, *Journal of a Soul,* Geoffrey Chapman, London, 1964, p. 144.)

Here we see evidence of how Roncalli in his journey to the priesthood was shaped by some of the wider historical, theological and cultural shifts in Catholicism. Roncalli's diary entry demonstrates his desire to remain faithful to the teaching of the Church while also responding to new historical circumstances.

As the young seminarian was facing these critical theological issues, he probably did not realise that he was becoming a true historian; for Roncalli was interpreting change.

Top Left: Pope John XXIII (middle) as a young student at the Pontifical Roman Seminary with two friends of the same home-town of Bergamo, 1901
Left: Pope John XXIII when he was Monsignor Roncalli, Bulgaria in 1927

Pope John XXIII—As Priest

Roncalli was ordained to the priesthood in Rome on 10 August 1904. There was speculation that he would remain in Rome to continue higher studies in canon law, but the appointment of a new bishop to Bergamo changed all that. Giacomo Radini Tedeschi (1857-1914) was consecrated as bishop of Bergamo personally by Pope Pius X in the Sistine Chapel on 29 January 1905. Roncalli assisted at the ceremony and was later chosen as the personal secretary of the bishop. On his return to Bergamo, Roncalli was occupied in two main tasks: lecturer in history at the diocesan seminary and secretary to Tedeschi. The new bishop modelled for his young secretary something that would be essential to Roncalli's later career; an emphasis on the bishop as pastor and shepherd, attentive to the needs of his people and seeking to bring about necessary adaptation of the diocese in the face of changing historical realities.

In order to familiarise himself with his new diocese, Tedeschi commenced an extensive program of pastoral visitation in Bergamo, which at the time numbered approximately 350 parishes. Working alongside the bishop, Roncalli began to develop an understanding of the essential link between pastoral activity and the process of renewal in the Church. The pastoral visitation culminated in a diocesan synod which was held in 1910. As secretary to the bishop, Roncalli was also appointed official secretary of the synod and responsible for publication of official documents. In a biography published soon after Tedeschi's death in 1914, Roncalli spoke of the synod as 'the most solemn and important event of his episcopate ... a source of intense joy'. It is important to note the way Roncalli framed his ideas historically and shaped a form of language that would have remarkable bearing on his decision, later as pope, to summon Vatican II:

> There had been no synod in Bergamo since 1724 – a gap of nearly two hundred years – so the occasion had special significance. The mass of old and new diocesan legislature which had been found here and there in innumerable documents, instructions, traditions and local customs, was revised,brought into line with the needs of modern times and altered circumstances and given new and authoritative confirmation. (A.G. Roncalli, *My Bishop: A Portrait of Mgr. Giacomo Radini Tedeschi* (translated by D. White, Geoffrey Chapman, London, 1969, p. 92.)

The phrase 'revised and brought into line with the needs of modern times' is a key phrase from the early writings of Roncalli that helps us to understand how history was shaping his perspective on the life and mission of the Church. The Italian word *aggiornamento* (bringing up-to-date) would later be used by John XXIII at Vatican II as a key idea of why he believed a council was necessary in order to respond to the rapid social, cultural and religious changes of the 1960s.

As Roncalli threw himself into his work as seminary lecturer and bishop's secretary, he found time to research and publish articles in the local Catholic journal *La Vita Diocesana* on the previous bishops of Bergamo, various diocesan synods and items of local history. But it was a chance discovery that would engage Roncalli's historical interest over a lifetime and, one could say, literally change the course of history. On a trip to Milan in 1906 with Tedeschi, Roncalli took himself off to the diocesan archives and made an accidental discovery. He found thirty-nine volumes of original material related to St Charles Borromeo's apostolic visitation to Bergamo in 1575 in the wake of the Council of Trent (1545-1563). The material was marked '*Archivio Spirituale – Bergamo*'. Roncalli later wrote:

> I was immediately struck by the collection of thirty-nine

> "Roncalli's later career [was]an emphasis on the bishop as pastor and shepherd, attentive to the needs of his people and seeking to bring about necessary adaptation of the diocese in the face of changing historical realities."

parchment volumes which I discovered and explored in great detail on subsequent visits. What a pleasant surprise to my spirit to find bound together such a copious and interesting collection of documents on the Church of Bergamo in a period of characteristic renewal following the Council of Trent ... (A.G. Roncalli, *Gli Atti della Visita Apostolica di San Carlo Borromeo a Bergamo* (1575), Vol. I, Firenze: Olschki, 1936.)

To understand why Vatican II was summoned in 1959, one needs to understand the importance of this discovery in 1906. These dusty and forgotten papers, centuries old, had activated something in Roncalli's historical imagination. While thousands of volumes have been written about Martin Luther and the Reformation, here Roncalli was captivated by what he believed was the *pastoral renewal* of the Church initiated by Borromeo in the wake of the Council of Trent. These dusty archives came alive in Roncalli's hands. Not only did they speak to him about some important past event; for Roncalli the historian the past had the capacity to also shape the present and the future.

Who was St Charles (or Carlo) Borromeo (1538-1584) and why is he important to Roncalli and the history of Vatican II? Borromeo was born of noble parentage in Arona, northwest of Milan, in 1538. He studied civil and canon law and was brought to Rome by his uncle Pope Pius IV and appointed secretary of state. He was named a cardinal at twenty-two years of age but not ordained a priest or bishop which was not uncommon at this time. Borromeo was named 'administrator' of the diocese of Milan and then became the city's archbishop in 1560 while continuing to work in Rome.
At the time, bishops were often appointed to numerous dioceses but hardly ever visited or resided in them. Following the death of his brother Federico, Charles was under pressure to use his position to protect the family's interests. It was at this time that he experienced a spiritual crisis. Charles was also aware of the 'reform' movements emanating from the Council of Trent and the express desire of the council that bishops reside in their dioceses and truly pastor those entrusted to their care. Borromeo chose to be ordained a priest and bishop; he left Rome and the privileged protection of his uncle and entered the city of Milan in 1565. He became the first resident bishop of Milan, the most ancient and prestigious diocese in Italy, in almost ninety years.

In Milan, Borromeo set about reforming the diocese through

Below left: Portrait of St Charles Borromeo (1538-1584), attributed to Giovanni Ambrogio Figino; created between 1575 and 1599

Below right: Council of Trent (1545-63)

extensive and systematic visitation of the parishes and through the convocation of eleven diocesan synods and six provincial councils. This was done to ensure that Trent's reform directives were made operative. He was a man of personal austerity and prayer who remained in Milan to care for victims of the plague while the nobility fled the city in fear. He built seminaries for the proper training of the clergy, issued directives for the restoration of churches that had fallen into decay, and published a manual on the importance of preaching. Borromeo demonstrated the link between the residence of bishops and the renewed effectiveness of pastoral ministry. When he undertook an extensive three-month visitation of the diocese of Bergamo in 1575, he left behind a significant archive of written instructions and directives for the pastoral good of the local Church. These papers had lain dormant for over three centuries until the young priest-historian, Angelo Roncalli, discovered them in Milan in 1906. Roncalli brought these papers to life.

Roncalli informed Bishop Tedeschi of his discovery. The bishop established a special commission to photograph, transcribe and edit the material for publication to coincide with the 300th anniversary of Borromeo's canonisation planned for 1910. By 1910, draft texts had been prepared. However, by 1914 Tedeschi was dead and World War I was about to break out. The new bishop of Bergamo showed little interest in this work and the commission was disbanded. However, Roncalli held onto the material and also the dream of one day seeing it published.

Did you know?

Prior to the Council of Trent, bishops had charge of numerous dioceses. Many bishops hardly ever stepped foot in their various dioceses but would leave the administration to delegates and other curial officials. Trent mandated that a bishop was to have charge of only one diocese, that he was to reside in that diocese, that he was to regularly visit the parishes of that diocese and that he was to establish a seminary for the proper formation of the clergy.

Pope John XXIII—As Bishop

In the early 1920s, Roncalli left Bergamo and was called to Rome and appointed National Director of the Missions. However, he was surprised in 1925 to learn that Pope Pius XI (1922-39) had selected him as Apostolic Visitor to Bulgaria. Roncalli had not undertaken formal training as a papal diplomat and was consecrated a bishop for the purposes of his new ministry. His association with Pius XI (Achille Ratti) was quite fortuitous. Ratti had been prefect of the Ambrosian Library in Milan and it was Ratti who both supervised and gave expert advice to the young Roncalli in copying and transcribing the papers of Borromeo's 1575 visitation that he had discovered in Milan in 1906.

Roncalli was consecrated a bishop on 19 March 1925 at the Church of San Carlo Borromeo in Rome. Roncalli set off to a largely unknown country with a very small and scattered Catholic population, vastly different from the world of Bergamo and Rome that had been familiar to him. But this important period in his life demonstrated a number of endearing features of Roncalli's personality – openness to new ideas, new experiences, new cultures and new historical circumstances. Roncalli's task in Bulgaria was to assess local conditions and report back to Rome. He thought his mission would last about six months and that he would then be transferred to a diocese of his own in Italy or a diplomatic appointment elsewhere. As time passed, Roncalli's diary and letters home hint at a certain sense of 'languishing' in Bulgaria. However he had always trusted God's will for his life and was under obedience to the pope.

During his time in Bulgaria, Roncalli would begin to finesse his own pastoral style of ministry, modelled very much on the historical figure of Borromeo and the example of Tedeschi. He undertook numerous visits to victims of a tragic earthquake in 1928 and distributed aid to

Catholics and non-Catholics alike which made a favourable impression on local authorities. As a young bishop, Roncalli constantly made reference to the essentially 'pastoral' nature of his ministry as a papal diplomat. There are photos of him riding on horseback to visit small and scattered Catholic communities in rural areas that had not seen a priest, let alone a bishop, in years. In a letter to his superiors in Rome, Roncalli spoke of 'a new era for the Catholic Church in the Orient ... a sign of the times'. Roncalli often worked towards positive, warm and friendly relations with the various branches of the Orthodox tradition and other non-Catholic communities, seeking to avoid the use of harsh language such as 'schismatics'.

Below: St Mark's, Venice

DID YOU KNOW?

During his time in Bulgaria, Roncalli spoke with great warmth and affection on the issue of ecumenism which became a hallmark of Vatican II.

I offer greetings and best wishes also to our separated Orthodox brothers (and sisters), separated from us because of diverse disciplinary reasons, but joined to us in the same adoration of Father, Son and Holy Spirit ... that one day, not too far from now, we will see ourselves united in the participation of peace and joy that the Holy Spirit, the Paraclete, pours out incessantly on the Catholic Church ...

Feast of Pentecost, Bulgaria, May 1925

"But this important period in his life demonstrated a number of endearing features of Roncalli's personality – openness to new ideas, new experiences, new cultures and new historical circumstances."

Pope John XXIII—As Nuncio

In 1934, Roncalli was advised by the Holy See that his new diplomatic posting would be to Turkey and Greece. He remained there throughout the Second World War and became known for his friendly and open attitude to non-Catholic Christians and adherents of the Muslim and Jewish faith. Members of the Jewish community in particular remember his efforts to protect them from the gas chambers of the Holocaust. It was during this time that Roncalli recommenced the work of editing the historical material on Borromeo that had been left in abeyance two decades earlier. In the slow and time-consuming task of editing this material, often late into the night, Roncalli started to see some parallels between Borromeo's pastoral reform in the wake of Trent in the sixteenth century and his diplomatic and pastoral ministry in the changing circumstances of the early twentieth century. As he went about the business of papal diplomacy and pastoral visitation, Roncalli often described this as 'the principal act of my ministry'.

In a remarkable burst of energy, Roncalli was able to publish three dense volumes of Borromeo's visitation. The Introduction to Volume 1 published in 1936 deserves particular attention. In outlining the pastoral renewal instigated by Trent and practiced by Borromeo, Roncalli describes this period as 'a fruitful rejuvenation of the Church ... a vigorous regaining of Catholic life ... an awakening of such potent energy not known in any other period of the Church'. Roncalli reserves a special place for Borromeo whom he praises for being a model bishop 'extending the benefits of his prodigious reforming activity throughout the parishes of the region'. Borromeo was thus recognised for his pastoral zeal and his ability 'to meet the new needs of the time'.

Why is this important? Why study the pastoral work of Borromeo in the wake of the Council of Trent and how could it be helpful to the modern-day Church? For Roncalli, two things were at play here. Firstly, historical scholarship and pastoral ministry were coming together. The editing of these historical papers was shaping Roncalli's language and style of ministry as a bishop. He constantly emphasised the 'pastoral' nature of his ministry as

Below: Cardinal Roncalli arrives in Venice in 1953.

a bishop and he would continue this emphasis, and indeed enhance it, following his election to the papacy in 1958. The other important thing to notice is that while Roncalli was acting as a bishop and papal diplomat, he never ceased being an historian. And what is the historian's task? To record and interpret change.

In 1944, Roncalli was transferred unexpectedly to the prestigious diplomatic post of Paris. He had now entered the upper echelons of Vatican diplomacy. But this promotion did not radically change the priest born of humble origins with a great interest in history. Roncalli's diary for this period shows consistent references to the essentially 'pastoral' nature of his diplomatic ministry, his dynamic view of history, and his sense that the Church and the world were entering 'new times' in the wake of the Second World War. At over sixty years of age, even in Paris and while on holidays in Italy, Roncalli would work late into the night to complete the fourth volume of Borromeo's visitation to be published in 1946.

This constant intersection between pastoral ministry and historical reflection continued when in 1953 Roncalli was appointed patriarch of Venice and nominated a cardinal. He had been away from his native Italy for almost thirty years and, one could say, he returned with a much more global sense of the Church and its mission. Roncalli was conscious that he now possessed what he had always desired – the direct care of souls as a diocesan bishop. Rather than relaxing into the splendour of the enchanting city of Venice, Roncalli commenced a prodigious round of pastoral visitation, describing himself constantly as the 'shepherd' and 'pastor' of the diocese. The extensive pastoral visitation of the diocese culminated in a diocesan synod in 1957. Roncalli knew the importance of synods in the life of the Church and had studied them closely. Diocesan synods and provincial councils were promoted in order to bring about renewal of the Church at the local level. As patriarch of Venice, Roncalli summoned his own synod and for the first time used the Italian word *aggiornamento*, indicating the need to bring things 'up-to-date'. At seventy-three years of age, Roncalli continued working on the fifth volume of Borromeo's 1575 pastoral visitation and this historical work continued to shape the language and style of Roncalli as pastor and historian.

Below: St Peter's Basilica, Rome

DID YOU KNOW?

It was at the diocesan synod in Venice in 1957 that Roncalli first used the word '*aggiornamento*'?

Haven't you heard the word 'aggiornamento' repeated many times? Here is our Church, always young and ready to follow the different changes in the circumstances of life, with the intention of adapting, correcting, improving, and arousing enthusiasm. In summary, this is the nature of the synod: this is its purpose.

Pope John XXIII—As Pope

In 1958, Pope Pius XII died after an eighteen-year reign. Prior to leaving for Rome, Roncalli wrote in his diary, 'The grace of the Lord is always with his Church. We are not on earth to look after a museum but to cultivate a flourishing garden of life and to prepare for a glorious future. The Pope is dead. Long live the Pope.' There was speculation in Rome about a successor and discussion of a 'transitional' or 'caretaker' pope for a short papacy where no major decisions or changes would be made. Roncalli was seen as that candidate – friendly, warm, genial and a relatively obscure and uncontroversial figure in the world of papal diplomacy who had an interest in 'history'.

Following his election on 28 October 1958, the Church and the world were immediately struck by the contrast of the new pope in comparison with his predecessor. There were many surprises. The first was the choice of name. The Church had been blessed by four 'Pius' popes in a hundred years. It was felt that the tradition would continue. When Roncalli announced 'John' as his papal designation, it took many by surprise. He stated that he chose John because it was the name of his father and the name of the humble parish of his baptism in Sotto il Monte. When was the last time a pope spoke so intimately of his father and the parish of his baptism? He also stated that John was the name of innumerable basilicas around the world, including his own Lateran Basilica as Bishop of Rome. He went on: 'It was the name of the long series of Roman pontiffs, all of whom had a short pontificate.'

The Church was not familiar with a newly elected pope speaking so warmly and intimately. If his choice of name indicated a new way of thinking, it was only the first of many innovations. In receiving the customary sign of respect from the cardinals following his election, John XXIII insisted that the custom of kissing the pontiff's feet, a gesture that had imperial overtones, should be eliminated immediately. Whereas Pius XII had appeared regal, serious and somewhat detached, John XXIII impressed many by his warm and down-to-earth character.

The new pope attempted to rid the Vatican of some of the exaggerated imperial overtones that had surrounded the papal office. As John XXIII began his new ministry, he gave subtle hints about the style of papacy he would follow. He spoke of being a shepherd and going out in search of the lost sheep. He insisted that his papal coronation was to be held on a feast day dear to his heart – November 4, the feast of St Charles Borromeo. The fifth and final volume of Borromeo's apostolic visitation was published soon after Roncalli's election to the papacy. Very few appreciated its historical significance.

Below: Pope John XXIII

Angelo Giuseppe Roncalli

1881 Born on 25 November in the small village of Sotto il Monte in Bergamo, in northern Italy

As a teenage seminarian, Roncalli commenced what would become his great spiritual testament, *Journal of a Soul.*

1901 Arrived in Rome (aged nineteen) to complete his studies for the priesthood

1904 Ordained to the priesthood in Rome on 10 August

1920s Left Bergamo and called to Rome and appointed National Director of the Missions

1925 Selected by Pope Pius XI to be Apostolic Visitor to Bulgaria

1925 Consecrated a bishop on 19 March at the church of San Carlo in Rome

1934 Advised by the Holy See that his new diplomatic posting would be to Turkey and Greece

1944 Transferred to the prestigious diplomatic post of Paris

1953 Appointed Patriarch of Venice

1958 Following his election on 28 October 1958, the Church and the world were immediately struck by the contrast of the new pope with his predecessor.

1962 The first session of the Council met from 11 October until 8 December 1962

1963 Pope John XXIII died on 3 June 1963.

The grace of the Lord is always with his Church.
We are not on earth to look after a museum
but to cultivate a flourishing garden of life
and to prepare for a glorious future.

Chapter 2

Calling the Council (Vatican II)

Pope John XXIII delivering a radio message, Spain, 21 October 1961

THE FIRST 100 DAYS

In contemporary discourse, much is made of a new leader's 'first 100 days'. Journalists watch for a change of direction or major policy shift in a new leader. The Roman Curia were just beginning to get used to the new and less formal style of John XXIII when a surprise announcement shocked many. It was 25 January 1959, the feast of the conversion of St Paul. John XXIII had just presided at the ceremony to close the Week of Prayer for Christian Unity, an observance dear to him following his time as papal diplomat in the Orient. Despite the sometimes frosty ecumenical relations before Vatican II, Rome observed this occasion with some formality. Following the celebration, John XXIII gathered a group of approximately twenty cardinals to the chapter house of the adjacent Benedictine monastery of St Paul Outside the Walls. The newly elected pope spoke for the first time as an historian and a pastor in dropping what could only be described as a bombshell:

> I am prompted to open my mind and heart to you and to tell you frankly about several points of planned pastoral activity which have emerged in my thoughts. In doing so, I am thinking of the care of the souls of the faithful in these modern times. As you know,

I have a double responsibility as both bishop of the Diocese of Rome and shepherd of the universal Church. First, let me reflect on the city of Rome. It is much changed since my own youth ...

Being a pastor responsible for the care of souls was something Roncalli learned in the first years of his priesthood at the side of Bishop Tedeschi in Bergamo. After decades of research on Borromeo in the wake of Trent, using a scholarly approach, he had diligently studied pastoral activity and the care of souls. In the early days of his papacy, John XXIII had noticed how much Rome had changed from his time as a student there in 1901. It was now a bustling post-war city of greater urbanisation. The historian-pope had noticed significant change and he wanted to engage with this process in a dynamic way. John XXIII continued:

So now, trembling a bit with emotion, I announce to you my intention to hold a twofold event: a diocesan wide meeting for this city and an ecumenical council for the universal Church. And this will also lead to a bringing-up-to-date of the code of canon law which will accompany and crown these two events ... We think this will produce a great enlightenment for all Christian people as well as a renewed invitation to our separated brothers and sisters (Bill Huebsch, *Vatican II in Plain English. The Council*, Thomas More Publishing, Allen, Texas, 1996, pp. 65-69.)

John XXIII would later say that his announcement was met with 'stony silence' by the cardinals. What strikes us about this section of his speech? A diocesan wide meeting for this city is formally called a synod. The Council of Trent encouraged bishops to regularly call synods and Borromeo was exemplary in ensuring that the pastoral reform decrees of Trent were made operative. Roncalli had studied this pastoral reform closely over the course of his life. In 1910, Bishop Tedeschi summoned a synod for the diocese of Bergamo and Roncalli stated that it was the most important initiative of the bishop given that a synod had not been held in Bergamo for almost two hundred years. Roncalli stated that the synod brought about great renewal of the Church at the local level and enabled the diocese to respond to changed historical circumstances. Now as pope, John XXIII had not forgotten his responsibility to the local diocese of Rome; in fact he wanted to enhance this responsibility. He wanted to act and speak like a diocesan bishop by convoking a synod. John XXIII wanted the diocese of Rome to undertake a conscious effort in pastoral renewal in order to respond to the changed historical circumstances of the city. Ironically, just like in Bergamo, there had not been a synod in Rome for almost two hundred years.

What type of council?

In announcing an ecumenical council for the Church, one needs to remember that councils give rise to great expectations. But what type of council? Was this the resumption of Vatican I suspended in an atmosphere of chaos in 1870 following the fall of the Papal States? Vatican I promulgated the teaching on papal infallibility. If a modern-day pope wanted to make changes in the Church, a council was not necessary. Papal infallibility was available. Historians now know that Pope Pius XI (1922-39) seriously toyed with the idea of resuming Vatican I. However, with the signing of the Lateran Treaty in 1929 and the recognition of Vatican sovereignty in international law, Pius XI left matters alone. In 1948, Pope Pius XII (1939-58) established a secret commission of cardinals to explore the idea of a council. This proposal made little progress. The council that John XXIII announced in January 1959 had no name. It was only in July 1959 that he announced that the council would be called 'Vatican II'. It would not simply be the resumption of the first Vatican Council of 1870. This would be an entirely different council; it would be a 'pastoral' council for meeting the changed needs of modern times.

Opposite page:
Opening of Council's 2nd Session
Vatican II in Rome

> "In announcing an ecumenical council for the Church, one needs to remember that councils give rise to great expectations."

Two other things are important to note. John XXIII announced the need to update (*aggiornamento*) the 1917 code of canon law. Four decades after its promulgation, the new pope felt that the code was not able to meet the needs of the Church. The pope used the word *aggiornamento* to 'update' the code of canon law in much the same way we update a publication, computer software or a website. By the time Vatican II commenced in 1962, many understood that John XXIII wanted to update the whole Church in its life and mission and not just the code of canon law. At the end of this announcement speech, John XXIII made it clear that his council would have a strong ecumenical focus on dialogue with other Christians. One wonders if the cardinals missed the importance of this point given that many were schooled in an understanding of ecumenism, whereby dissident or schismatic denominations simply 'returned' to the Church of Rome.

Preparing the council was a massive undertaking. Senior figures in the Roman Curia wanted to send out a formulated questionnaire to the bishops of the world. John XXIII insisted that the bishops were to 'freely' offer suggested themes or ideas for discussion at the council. This idea of bishops speaking freely took on particular significance once the council started in terms of them finding their voice, often in the midst of intense debates. Many bishops sought out the advice of theologians, seminary rectors and ecclesiastical academics. A number of these scholars gave advice that built on many decades of research and scholarship in theology and pastoral practice. For example, many promoted a more historical and critical understanding of the scriptures and an enhanced and better liturgical participation of the faithful. There were ideas such as the promotion of the authentic and distinctive vocation of laity based on their baptism, enhanced dialogue and interaction with non-Catholic and non-Christian organisations.

The process of worldwide consultation and the assembly of preparatory documents or schemata took almost three years. Some less enlightened bishops wanted the council to condemn and denounce communism, to issue new Marian decrees and to address technical points of canon law. The logistical arrangements of the council were just as complex as the theological ones. Rome was on standby to receive almost 2,500 bishops from around the world with their secretaries and advisers, and a large international media contingent that, with the advent of television, began to take serious interest in this major gathering of Catholic bishops.

A global gathering

After almost four years of intense preparation, Vatican II commenced on 11 October 1962. Prior to the commencement of the council, a long procession of bishops made their way into St Peter's Basilica. Many observers were struck not simply by the sheer number of bishops but by the diversity of their background and appearance. There were bishops from Asia, Africa, Latin America and Oceania as well as bishops from the various Eastern rite and Oriental traditions of the Catholic Church – Melkites, Maronites, Ukrainians, Chaldeans, Syro-Malabars, Coptics and Armenians. This was not simply a manifestation of unity in diversity; it was a powerful demonstration of the true universality and catholicity of the Church. It also demonstrated a truly global gathering of bishops to consider the pressing global issues of the era.

> “American theologian Jared Wicks SJ described the pope's speech as 'the council's first great text'.”

At the end of the procession

came John XXIII, carried on the *sedia gestatoria*. He looked somewhat worried and pensive. There had been many disagreements in the wording of the almost seventy preparatory schemata. Many did not know that the pope had been diagnosed with stomach cancer. After stepping down from the throne, John XXIII intoned the hymn to the Holy Spirit, Mass was celebrated in Latin and the bishops recited the Profession of Faith. Many would have noticed the Book of the Gospels solemnly enthroned before them as had been done at previous councils. Not only did this recall the sovereignty of Christ over the gathering but it would also lead to Vatican II's renewed appreciation of the place of the word of God in the life of Catholics. After almost three hours of various liturgical observances, the pope commenced his formal address.

The papal address

Gaudet Mater Ecclesia – Holy Mother Church rejoices! … John XXIII began his Latin address in a firm and clear voice. Unlike most papal speeches and discourses which are written by advisers and specialists, this papal address was written personally by the pope over the course of many weeks with many revisions. In reminding all of his peasant background, he describes the address as 'flour from my own sack'. Vatican II was 'his' council and this opening address was going to be foundational in terms of giving the council inspiration and direction. American theologian Jared Wicks SJ described the pope's speech as 'the council's first great text'.

The address is best remembered for the way John XXIII hit out at 'the prophets of doom', members of the Roman Curia who carried on as if everything in life was heading towards disaster and ruin. The pope noted that these people 'are full of zeal but lacking a sense of discretion and measure'. The pope stated that these times are no worse than previous eras and he reminded his audience that 'history is the teacher of life'. John XXIII reminded the bishops that Vatican II would be a fundamentally 'pastoral' council concerned with bringing the Church up-to-date with the needs of modern times. Vatican II was not summoned to argue about particular points of theology or to condemn modern errors. The pope wanted the council to teach more effectively, to promote Christian unity and to be attentive to the global implications of a new epoch of human history. In the Church's teaching role not just to Catholics but to all of humanity, John XXIII insisted that 'today we prefer to make use of the medicine of mercy rather than that of severity'. He wanted the Church to teach in a different way, hence his statement that 'the substance of our central beliefs is one thing and the way it is presented is another'.

Opposite page: Members of hierarchy meet. Vatican II 1963, © MDHC Catholic Archdiocese of Melbourne

Below: Bishop of Wa from Ghana and Pope John XXIII at the Second Vatican Council

“John XXIII insisted that 'today we prefer to make use of the medicine of mercy rather than that of severity'. He wanted the Church to teach in a different way, hence his statement that 'the substance of our central beliefs is one thing and the way it is presented is another'.”

The First Session of Vatican II

In his opening address, John XXIII alluded to the fact that there would be debate and disagreements at the council with the statement that 'everything, even human differences, leads to a greater good for the Church'. The historian knew this from his study of previous councils and was not afraid. In fact, despite the growing centralisation of papal power, John XXIII made an extraordinary statement of trust in the sense of collegiality that Vatican II would rediscover in stressing, 'The Church is now in your hands'. The full implications of this statement were about to be played out in dramatic fashion. Before Vatican II got down to business, bishops needed to be elected to various commissions. The curia had prepared a list of hand-picked candidates that they thought the council fathers would simply rubber-stamp. They were seriously mistaken, as the bishops demonstrated their independence of thought and action. (A similar resistance to curial expectations of rubber-stamping occurred at Vatican I in 1869). Cardinal Liénart of France dramatically moved a motion requesting that the bishops have time to consider the lists of names and to make amendments. He was seconded by Cardinal Frings of Germany, whose theological adviser or *peritus* was a young theologian called Joseph Ratzinger. The bishops endorsed the motion of Liénart and Frings by vigorous applause and a vote in favour. The session was suspended as the bishops streamed out of St Peter's Basilica and gathered in national groups. The first flashpoint!

Of all the preparatory schemata, the bishops felt that the one on the liturgy was the most suitable for initial debate. The first question that came up was the issue of Latin in the liturgy. While John XXIII had reaffirmed the importance of Latin for seminary studies, many bishops, especially in mission countries, felt that the possibility of vernacular languages in the liturgy fulfilled John XXIII's exhortation of the need to 'adapt to new and changed historical circumstances'. Conservatives railed against any change to Latin as they spoke of its enduring value to the Church's universality. Despite their scholastic formation, as

Below: Bishops' procession in the Basilica of St Peter at the opening of the Second Vatican Council, Rome, Italy, 1962

■ Cardinal Alfredo Ottaviani – secretary of the Holy Office and president of the Preparatory Theological Commission; generally seen as the leading figure of the minority of the council.

■ Cardinal Giuseppe Siri – archbishop of Genoa and member of the Central Preparatory Commission, spokesman for the minority and close adviser to Pope Pius XII. Is alleged to have said that the idea of the council was John XXIII's 'fifteen minutes of folly'.

■ Cardinal Augustin Bea – German Jesuit and brilliant scripture scholar, later to become president of the Secretariat for Christian Unity, a cause very dear to John XXIII's heart. Bea was confessor to Pope Pius XII and helped to shape Catholic openness to critical biblical studies.

■ Maximos IV Saigh – Patriarch of Antioch (Syria) and leader of the Melkite bishops at the council. Noted for his outspoken comments in terms of reminding council fathers of the rich, ancient and diverse Eastern and Oriental traditions of the Catholic Church.

■ Cardinal Joseph Frings – archbishop of Cologne and leading spokesman for the majority. His young theological adviser at the council was none other than Joseph Ratzinger (Pope Benedict XVI).

■ Cardinal Leon-Joseph Suenens – archbishop of Malines/Brussels, one of the most influential members of the council and highly influential in the framing of the document *Gaudium et Spes*.

■ Cardinal Giovanni Battista Montini – archbishop of Milan, elected as Pope Paul VI in 1963 following the death of John XXIII. Highly gifted thinker who as pope had to hold in tension the many factions of the council.

■ Cardinal Giacomo Lercaro – archbishop of Bologna, leading proponent of liturgical and catechetical renewal after the council. Was instrumental in co-founding Bologna's Institute of Religious Sciences in the early 1950s in order to promote theological and historical renewal in the Church before Vatican II.

■ Archbishop Marcel Lefebvre – French-born African missionary, former superior general of the Holy Ghost Fathers and archbishop of Dakak (Senegal). Implacable opponent of many of Vatican II's reforms who was excommunicated in 1988 for illicitly ordaining four bishops without a mandate from the Holy See.

■ Edward Schillebeeckx – Belgian Dominican theologian and adviser to Cardinal Alfrink of Utrecht. Leading light in terms of renewing the Church's understanding of the sacraments and Christian anthropology.

■ Yves Congar – French Dominican theologian who promoted major ecclesiological renewal for the Church and who was censured by Rome before Vatican II. His ideas gained wide acceptance even in the face of great resistance from the minority.

■ Joseph Ratzinger – brilliant young German theologian, professor at Bonn then Munster, theological adviser to Cardinal Frings. Highly influential among the German bishops and generally considered in the vanguard of promoting reform and renewal in theology. As cardinal and head of the Congregation for the Doctrine of the Faith (CDF) in Rome, perceived as putting the 'brakes' on some of Vatican II's reforms.

■ Karl Rahner – German Jesuit theologian, under suspicion before the council but named by John XXIII as consultant to the Preparatory Commission on the Sacraments and personal adviser to Cardinal Koenig of Vienna. A prolific author and highly significant theologian of the twentieth century,

■ Marie-Dominique Chenu – French Dominican theologian and historian, founder of 'la nouvelle théologie'– new methods of understanding theology that were highly criticized by Rome before Vatican II.

■ Jean Danielou – French Jesuit theologian, early promoter of 'la nouvelle théologie' whose work mainly focused on the Church's relationship to the world. Was later appointed as cardinal, and was less than positive about some of Vatican II's outcomes.

■ Henri de Lubac – French Jesuit theologian and historian, censured before the council for promoting critical historical studies on the Church, also later made a cardinal.

■ John Courtney Murray – American Jesuit theologian, expert on Church/State relations, censured before the council by Rome but highly influential in the drafting of *Dignitatis Humanae* and expert on issues of religious liberty and conscience.

■ Johannes Willebrands – Dutch priest who after Bea was the leading light in the Secretariat for Christian Unity and a giant in the ecumenical world after the council.

■ Jean Guitton – French Catholic layman, philosopher and theologian, close friend and adviser to Paul VI but named one of the first lay auditors by John XXIII. Guitton had met Roncalli during the latter's time as nuncio in Paris.

bishops got up to speak many could not understand each other's Latin. Maximos Saigh, the Melkite Patriarch, stood up and spoke in French. He reminded the council fathers that many of the Eastern and Oriental traditions spoke a range of ancient liturgical languages. Latin was normative for the Roman, western and European tradition of Catholicism. However, the diverse Eastern and Oriental traditions were undeniably Catholic in their communion with the Holy See and the successor of Peter, but do not have Latin as their normative liturgical and theological language. Saigh stated, 'Christ after all spoke the language of his contemporaries ... all languages are liturgical'.

The first session of the council met from 11 October until 8 December 1962. There was much discussion over the document on the liturgy as well as other documents such as those on divine revelation, social communication and the schema on the Church. After this long eight-week period, no documents were formally approved but instead all were subject to further review and revision. The first session closed and would reconvene one year later.

Death of the Pope

Prior to the commencement of the second session, John XXIII died on 3 June 1963. It was the eve of Pentecost, a feast dear to the heart of the late pope who had called Vatican II 'a new Pentecost' for the Church. There was universal grief and mourning, including among non-Catholics and non-Christians, over the death of this much-loved pope. According to canon law, the council was technically suspended subject to the intentions of the new pope who was under no obligation to continue what John XXIII had started. On 21 June 1963, Giovanni Battista Montini, the cardinal archbishop of Milan was elected, took the name of Paul VI and immediately announced that Vatican II would reconvene.

It was Paul VI who steered the council through an increasingly turbulent period of discussion and debate and often had to contend with the demands of two opposing forces, the majority and the minority, sometimes also called progressives and traditionalists. Any concession granted to one group was often resisted by the other. Paul VI was an entirely different leader to John XXIII. Paul VI worried incessantly, checked drafts of documents carefully with his red pencil, at times appeared indecisive and took criticism very personally. John XXIII had been much more genial and spontaneous. Paul VI, steeped in European culture and learning, at times appeared to have the weight of the Church and the world upon his shoulders. All sixteen

Right: Cardinal Roncalli and Archbishop Giovanni Battista Montini of Milan

Opposite page left: Pope Paul VI (1963-78)

Opposite page right: Joseph Ratzinger and Yves Congar

final documents of Vatican II were formally approved under Paul VI's leadership. Despite the sometimes intense nature of debate, there was overwhelming endorsement in the final votes.

Despite his personality, Paul VI, like his predecessor, significantly reshaped the office of the papacy. Having taken the name of St Paul, the great missionary and apostle to the nations, Paul VI continued what John XXIII had begun – a renewed papacy building bridges to the modern world. As Vatican II unfolded, it was Paul VI who heard the call of Cardinal Suenens from Belgium in terms of allowing lay auditors into the council, including women. In 1965, Paul VI was the first pope to address the United Nations, and he did so pleading for an end to all war as the conflict in Vietnam spiralled out of control. In January 1964, Paul VI met the Ecumenical Patriarch Athenagoras in a warm encounter that attempted to heal centuries of division between the Roman Catholic Church and the Orthodox. In 1960 John XXIII had a 'private' meeting with the Anglican archbishop of Canterbury, Geoffrey Fisher, in a truly historic encounter. No pope and Anglican leader had met since the Reformation. In 1966, Paul VI went one step further in his meeting with archbishop Michael Ramsay. The Catholic pope placed an episcopal ring on the finger of the Anglican leader. While doctrinal and disciplinary differences still remain with the Orthodox and many Protestants, the ecumenical impulse of Vatican II brought down many walls of historic barriers and divisions.

In the wake of the council, the Church promoted a more humble style of leadership and a commitment of genuine solidarity with the poor. In 1963, Paul VI was crowned with the papal 'tiara', a medieval symbol denoting his universal power and jurisdiction. He directed that it be sold and the money given to the poor. Not only did Paul VI refuse to subsequently wear another tiara but each of his successors has done away with this symbol. The custom now is that each new pope inaugurates his ministry with the simple placing of the pallium, the woollen band marked with crosses, over his shoulders.

Paul VI continued what John XXIII had begun – a renewed papacy building bridges to the modern world.

Vatican II – The Australian Contribution

When John XXIII announced the council in January 1959, the Roman curia wanted to send a formal questionnaire to the world's bishops. John XXIII overruled the curia and insisted that the bishops 'speak freely' of their thoughts, desires and ideas for the coming council. Some bishops immediately consulted theologians and put together ideas on many of the burning issues of the preceding decades – renewal of the liturgy, ecumenism, Catholics and the Bible, reform of seminaries, promoting the vocation of the laity, and issues relating to justice, peace, poverty and economic development.

> "Archbishop Guilford Young of Hobart was by far the standout figure among his colleagues."

In Australia the response from bishops was mixed. Cardinal Norman Gilroy of Sydney recommended an examination of canon law related to marriage, and dispensations able to be granted by bishops. Bishop James O'Collins of Ballarat consulted his senior priests and stated that 'all was well in his diocese' and did not think it wise to make suggestions to the Holy See. Bishop Goody of Bunbury recommended serious ecumenical considerations and a view to possibly restoring the permanent diaconate to married men. Bishop Thomas Cahill of Cairns insisted on clerical dress for priests. Bishop Patrick Farrelly of Lismore recommended that priests use adequately paid pastoral assistants in the work of parish visitation. Bishop Andrew Tynan of Rockhampton suggested a detailed look at the lay apostolate. And many bishops recommended a simplification of the breviary, devotions to the Blessed Virgin Mary, and other matters to do with the administration of the sacraments.

Archbishop Guilford Young of Hobart was by far the standout figure among his colleagues. For many years, Young had been advocating a vernacular liturgy and increased participation by the faithful, an enhancement of the vital role of laity, and a renewed appreciation of the sacramental mystery of the Church. Young had been closely reading the work of French Dominican theologian Yves Congar. At ninety-five years of age, Archbishop Daniel Mannix of Melbourne did not make an initial submission in 1959. However, once Vatican II commenced, Mannix made a prophetic critique of the preparatory schema *De Ecclesia*, later to become the key document of Vatican II on the Church, *Lumen Gentium*. In 1963, Mannix suggested that the initial document was too scholastic, emphasised excessively the juridical and institutional dimensions of the Church, ignored the rich imagery of scripture and the early fathers, and did not give adequate recognition to the importance of laity.

Did you know?

At ninety-nine years of age, Archbishop Daniel Mannix of Melbourne issued a stern critique of *De Ecclesia*, the Council's preparatory document on the Church? He said:

The Schema smacks more of a legal document than a spiritual proclamation of religious faith ... for it treats too much of the juridical aspects of the Church, which is almost exclusively represented as a juridical society rather than a participation in the sacrament hidden from the world in God ... The Schema is too preoccupied with the rule and rights of the Church desiring power and authority ... The 'data' of the schema seem to be more recent pontifical sentences rather than the Word of God in Sacred Scripture and the writings of the Fathers ... No other function is seen to be allotted to the laity in the Church than carrying out the commands of the Hierarchy...It is demanded that the Council affirm more clearly that authority in the Church is humble service and ministry to all... (Jeffrey Murphy, "The Lost (and Last) Animadversions of Daniel Mannix", Australasian Catholic Record, Vol. LXXVI, no. 1, January 1999, p. 70.)

Rosemary Goldie

By far the most outstanding Australian contribution to Vatican II was not the work of a bishop or priest. Rosemary Goldie (1916-2010) studied arts at the University of Sydney and then travelled on a scholarship to the prestigious Sorbonne in Paris in 1936 where she obtained an MA. In Paris, Goldie was exposed to the intellectual world of Europe and became acquainted with the developing theology of Catholic Action and the lay apostolate as promoted by Pius XI. Catholic Action had commenced earlier that century by the young Belgian priest Joseph Cardijn (later a cardinal) who was concerned about the alienation of Catholic youth from the local parish. Cardijn had formed the Young Christian Workers (YCW) which became a major youth movement in Australia based on the model of see-judge-act. Goldie was familiar with many European currents of thought that prepared the way for Vatican II such as the lay apostolate, reform of the liturgy and ecumenism.

In Paris, Goldie was associated with Veritas, a small group of Catholic women students at the Sorbonne and Pax Romana, the international organisation of Catholic university students. Goldie had also come to know members of the Grail movement, an international organisation of active Catholic lay women. Goldie returned to Sydney to teach and towards the end of the Second World War in 1945 returned to Paris to commence a doctorate on French literature. Goldie put aside the doctorate and worked full time for Pax Romana, attended UNESCO and was a delegate in 1951 to the First World Congress of the Laity in Rome. Goldie's intellectual gifts were recognised when in 1952 she moved to Rome to work for the Permanent Committee for International Congresses of the Lay Apostolate. It was during this time that Goldie came to know a Vatican official named Monsignor Giovanni Battista Montini, the future Paul VI.

When John XXIII announced Vatican II in 1959, Goldie and her associates were literally 'on the spot' and took an active interest in the council's themes and preparation. When Vatican II commenced in 1963, various leaders of churches and denominations came to Rome as observers and honoured guests. John XXIII had invited noted French lay Catholic intellectual, Jean Guitton (1901-1999). However, Guitton was seen as an 'oddity' and placed with the ecumenical observers! Later, lay male auditors were appointed to the council and only in 1964 did Paul VI appoint the first group of female auditors. As the council considered both the mystery of the Church (*Lumen Gentium*), the relationship of the Church to the modern world (*Gaudium et Spes*), and a specific document on the laity (*Apostolicam Actuositatem*), it was Cardinal Suenens of Belgium (1904-1996) who made the cryptic comment, 'Women too should be invited as auditors. Unless I am mistaken, they make up half the human race'.

Suenens was not a lone voice crying in the wilderness. Before the council, Archbishop Philip Pocock of Toronto (1906-1984) not only consulted priests and theologians but lay men and women also, and took the suggestions of the latter very seriously.

Below: Rosemary with a bishop during Vatican II

Women in the Church

Bishop Alexander Carter (1909-2002) of Ontario complained that lay people had been consulted 'too little, too late' and that some of the preparatory documents 'had been conceived in the original sin of clericalism'. Archbishop Paul Hallinan (1911-1968) of Atlanta spoke out strongly against the 'subordinate' place of women in

the Church. Suenens petitioned Paul VI, and Goldie and other women were appointed as official non-voting auditors at the Second Vatican Council. While laymen had officially attended earlier councils as royal envoys and imperial representatives, Vatican II was the first time in history that women had a role in its proceedings.

Lay auditors attended all ceremonies in St Peter's Basilica, had access to the preparatory documents, and attended morning sessions with the bishops called 'congregations' and afternoon meetings of the conciliar sub-commissions. As laity they had no voting rights, however many bishops and theologians wanted their comments on areas of life that the council wished to touch on such as the lay apostolate, family life, issues of war, peace, justice and development, international politics and matters of economic concern. So impressive was Rosemary Goldie that in the wake of Vatican II, Paul VI established a new department in the Roman Curia called the Pontifical Council for the Laity. Goldie was appointed its undersecretary, the first time a woman had been appointed to such a senior position in the Vatican bureaucracy. Goldie held that position until 1976 when, ironically, she was succeeded by a priest. She then became a professor of theology at the Pontifical Lateran University, returned to Sydney to retire, and in 1990 was awarded an Order of Australia for service to religion and international relations. She died in 2010 and left a remarkable international and intellectual legacy.

In her 1996 book *Guests in Their Own House*, Carmel McEnroy amplifies the extraordinary contribution of Goldie and the other twenty-two women from fourteen different countries appointed as auditors at Vatican II. McEnroy argues forcefully that the women auditors were not at the council for simple 'decoration' or to satisfy a clerical desire for a symbolic, though silent, female presence. The lay auditors, especially the women, had intellectual gifts and a specific skill set of life experience that the council fathers needed to hear. For example, the first woman to enter the council was Marie-Louise Monnet (1902-1988), French foundress of the International Movement for the Apostolate in Independent Social Milieux, who became involved with Catholic Action based on her contact with the YCW. Of the others who were admitted, Pilar Bellosillo from Spain was president of the World Union of Catholic Women's Organisations and Alda Miceli was president of the Italian Women's Centre. Gladys Parentelli from Uruguay was vice-president of the female branch of the International Movement of Catholic Agricultural and Rural Youth, while French sister Suzanne Guillemin was superior general of the Daughters of Charity. Luz

> "Rosemary Goldie was universally recognised as a 'walking encyclopaedia' on the international lay apostolate, French theology and ecumenical movements, hence her unique appointment as undersecretary of the Pontifical Council for the Laity in 1967."

Alvarez-Icaza and her husband José from Mexico were the only married couple admitted as lay auditors.

Sr Mary Luke Tobin was the superior general of the American Sisters of Loretto and president of the Conference of Major Religious Superiors of the USA. Feisty and outspoken, Tobin could not wait to launch into her work at Vatican II for she felt that all the women had a unique contribution to make. Tobin tells the story that when she attended the office that issued identity cards for admission to the council, a rather imperious Vatican official stated, 'Remember, Sister, you are only entitled to attend those sessions that have direct bearing on your apostolate'. Tobin thought to herself, 'Good, I'll go to all of them!'

The intellectual and international backgrounds of the women listed above challenged the sometimes preconceived and traditional notions many of the bishops had of women. Basically, women were either religious or mothers and supported the Church's ministry as housekeepers, church cleaners and flower arrangers. The presence of the female auditors at Vatican II was both prophetic, challenging, frustrating and sometimes difficult. Sadly, normal courtesies and simple politeness were overlooked. Many bishops simply walked past the women and ignored them. Some council fathers, in a rhetorical flourish, spoke of them in idealised portraits of womanhood and femininity with phrases such as 'admirable sisters' and 'beautiful flowers'. Two coffee bars were installed inside St Peter's Basilica for the benefit of the bishops. Male auditors could mingle freely with the bishops but the female auditors were whisked away to a separate section. Even the married couple from Mexico could not enjoy a coffee together. Once these 'misunderstandings' were ironed-out, both the male and female auditors got down to the serious business of the council. Paul VI had invited them because as laity 'they were experts in life' and many bishops and theologians interacted with them, discussed the various draft documents and listened attentively to the laity's suggestions and recommendations.

Of the twenty-three women auditors, nineteen were single, three were widows, one was married and they represented fourteen nations of the world. Patrick Keegan of Great Britain, International President of the YCW, was the first lay person to address the council formally on 13 October 1964. Sadly, by the close of the council the following year, none of the female auditors had been given the same privilege. However, Rosemary Goldie was universally recognised as a 'walking encyclopaedia' on the international lay apostolate, French theology and ecumenical movements, hence her unique appointment as undersecretary of the Pontifical Council for the Laity in 1967.

The presence of all the lay auditors heralded a new awareness of the dignity and grace of the lay vocation in the life of the Church, not by virtue of privilege granted or special invitation, but by virtue of the sacramental grace of baptism and confirmation. Even the specific references to women in the Vatican documents looks tame by contemporary standards. However, the Rubicon had been crossed and there was no turning back:

> Since in our days women are taking an increasingly active share in the whole life of society, it is very important that their participation in the various sectors of the Church's apostolate should likewise develop (Decree on the Apostolate of the Laity, *Apostolicam Actuositatem*, no. 9).

Above: Rosemary presents John Paul II with a copy of her book *From a Roman Window*, watched by Cardinal Cassidy

Opposite: Rosemary with other auditors during Vatican II

THE SECOND VATICAN COUNCIL: A TIME LINE

1959

Council events
Jan 25: Pope John XXIII announces his intention of calling an ecumenical council.

World events
- Fidel Castro becomes premier of Cuba
- Joan Miró does the murals for the UNESCO Building in Paris
- Formal construction of the Sydney Opera House began
- Donald Bradman retires from cricket

1960

Council
June 5: Preparatory commissions and secretariats for the council set up by *motu proprio*, meaning under the pope's personal authority.

World
- John F Kennedy elected president of the United States
- Three women admitted to the ministry of the Swedish Lutheran church
- Arthur Calwell becomes the leader of the Australian Labor Party

1961

Council
Dec. 25: The council is formally summoned by the apostolic constitution *Humanae Salutis*.

World
- President John F Kennedy inaugurates the Peace Corps
- UN General Assembly condemns apartheid
- Berlin Wall constructed
- Meeting of the World Council of Churches in Delhi
- Yuri Gagarin (USSR) orbits the earth.

1962

Council
Sept. 5: Norms and procedures of the council settled by the apostolic constitution *Appropinquante Concilio*
Oct. 11-Dec. 8: First session of the council meets

World
- Cuban missile crisis
- Australian Army advisers sent to Vietnam to assist in training parts of the South Vietnamese army
- Robert Menzies' *Commonwealth Electoral Act* provided that all Aboriginal Australians should have the right to enrol and vote at federal elections

THE SECOND VATICAN COUNCIL: A TIME LINE

1963

Council

June 3: Pope John XXIII dies
June 21: Pope Paul VI elected; announces to continue the council
Sept. 29-Dec. 4: Second session of the council meets
Dec. 4: *Sacrosanctum concilium*, "Constitution on the Sacred Liturgy"; *Inter Mirifica*, "Decree On the Means of Social Communication"

World

- Civil rights demonstrations in Birmingham, AL, culminate in the arrest of Martin Luther King Jr. and the calling out of 3,000 troops by President Kennedy
- Nuclear test ban treaty signed by the United States, Soviet Union and Great Britain
- President John F. Kennedy is assassinated
- Australia signs a trade agreement with Japan
- *Yolngu* people petition the Australian House of Representatives with a bark petition after the government sold part of the Arnhem Land reserve on 13 March to a bauxite mining company
- Daniel Mannix, Archbishop of Melbourne dies

1964

Council

Jan. 4-6: Pope Paul VI meets Ecumenical Patriarch Athenagoras in the Holy Land
May 17: Secretariat for Non-Christian Religions established
Sept. 14-Nov. 21: Third session of the council meets
Issued on Nov. 21: *Lumen Gentium*, "Dogmatic Constitution On the Church"; *Orientalium Ecclesiarum*, "Decree On the Catholic Churches of the Eastern Rite"; *Unitatis Redintegratio*, "Decree on Ecumenism"

World

- Martin Luther King Jr wins the Nobel Peace Prize
- Prime Minister Robert Menzies announces the reintroduction of National Service
- The first edition of *The Australian* newspaper published in Canberra

Left: Sydney Opera House, plaque honouring Martin Luther King Jr; John XXIII with prisoners, Archbishop Mannix with Sir Robert Menzies, ©MDHC Catholic Archdiocese of Melbourne, Berlin wall

THE SECOND VATICAN COUNCIL: A TIME LINE

1965

Council

Sept. 14- Dec. 8: Fourth session of the council meets

Sept. 15: Pope Paul VI issues an apostolic constitution, *Apostolica Sollicitudo*, which formulates norms for a new episcopal synod established to assist the pope in governing the church

Oct. 28: *Christus Dominus*, "Decree Concerning the Pastoral Office of Bishops in the Church"; *Perfectae Caritatis*, "Decree On Renewal of Religious Life"; *Optatam Totius*, "Decree On Priestly Training"; *Gravissimum Educationis*, "Declaration On Christian Education"; *Nostra Aetate*, "Declaration On the Relation of the Church to Non-Christian Religions"

Nov. 18: *Dei Verbum*, "Dogmatic Constitution On Divine Revelation"; *Apostolicam Actuositatem*, "Decree On the Apostolate of the Laity"

Dec. 4: Prayer Service for Promoting Christian Unity held at St. Paul Outside the Walls

Dec. 7: *Dignitatis Humanae*, "Declaration On Religious Freedom"; *Ad Gentes*, "Decree on the Mission Activity of the Church"; *Presbyterorum Ordinis*, "Decree on the Ministry and Life of Priests"; *Gaudium et Spes*, "Pastoral Constitution on the Church In the Modern World"

Dec. 8: The Second Vatican Council is solemnly ended; extraordinary Jubilee Year proclaimed to familiarise the faithful with the teachings of the council

World

- Pope Paul VI addresses U.N. assembly in New York
- Prime Minister Menzies commits the first regular military forces to serve in combat in Vietnam
- Aboriginal Australians gain right to vote in state of Queensland
- Charles Perkins leads The Freedom Ride
- The first drawing of the National Service conscription lottery

Silent Demonstration

ADELAIDE. — Methodist and Congregationalist theological students joined aborigines in a "silent demonstration" outside the Norwood Oval before the football match of the day on a recent Saturday.

The demonstration was led by Mr. Joe McGuiness, president of the Federal Council for the Advancement of Aborigines and Torres Strait Islanders, and the Rev. A. H. M. Ellison (Methodist) of Magill, a former N.T. missionary.

Mr. McGuiness, joint director with Mr. Gordon Bryant, M.P., of the national vote "Yes" for aboriginal rights committee, is touring Australia speaking on aboriginal rights before the 27 May referendum.

• Here a small aboriginal boy admires the placard Mr. McGuiness holds during the demonstration.

Placards read: "All Parliament says YES", "Australia's Catholic Bishops say YES", "The Council of Churches says YES", and "All Australians must say YES for aboriginal rights".

About 40 theological students and members of the Young Liberals and Young Labour Contingent took part in the demonstration.

They handed out leaflets asking Australians to say YES to the referendum question asking that clauses discriminating against aborigines be removed from the Australian Constitution.

Above: Joe McGuiness, silent demonstration Adelaide, *The Advocate* 11 May 1967

Chapter 3

Implementing Vatican II

Once the council concluded on 8 December 1965, and all the bishops returned home, the task of implementing Vatican II across the world began, albeit somewhat unevenly. Some dioceses were slow to move whereas others moved quickly in terms of informing the faithful, making available easy-to-read translations and guides of the documents, and assembling numerous inservice meetings of clergy, religious and laity. The most tangible and immediate change that touched the lives of ordinary Catholics concerned the liturgy. Not only was the liturgy the first document debated by the bishops, it was the one that demonstrated fairly early the Church's capacity to put in place directives of the council in terms of the vernacular, lay participation and changes to church architecture and design.

The first shock for many average Catholics was seeing the priest facing them directly and hearing the parts of the Mass spoken in English rather than Latin. Prior to the council, when the priest said in Latin at the high altar *Dominus vobiscum* (The Lord be with you), the altar boy to the side of him answered quietly, *Et cum spirito tuo* (And with your spirit). Once the changes were implemented, the priest was now closer to the people, faced the congregation, and his greeting 'The Lord be with you' required a communal response from all those present as the council fathers intended.

Temporary altars were set up closer to the congregation, the altar rails dividing the sanctuary from the main body of the church were removed, and for the first time in centuries, women were allowed to enter the sanctuary area and proclaim the word of God. Lay people were allowed to assist the priest in the distribution of communion and the Eucharist was now available 'under both species'. The host could now be received on the hand rather than the previous practice of receiving it on the tongue while kneeling. Other liturgical actions which we take for granted today were unknown before Vatican II, such as the laity reading the prayers of the faithful and the procession of the gifts of bread and wine to the altar.

Many welcomed the changes; others found them totally confronting. Although the changes appeared as 'revolutionary', they were in fact the recovery of liturgical practices that had been part of the early tradition of the Church but long ignored. Scholars had recovered the early liturgical practices of the patristic era. Vatican II insisted that the liturgy and the sacraments were not 'private' functions of the priest, where the people sat passively saying the rosary or following the Mass in their own missals. The document on the liturgy (*Sacrosanctum Concilium*) indicates this change of mentality:

> Pastors of souls must, therefore, realise that, when the liturgy is celebrated, obligation goes further than simply ensuring that the laws governing valid and lawful celebration are observed. They must also ensure that the faithful take part fully aware of what they are doing, actively engaged in the rite and enriched by it (no.11).

Changes to the liturgy

The most obvious and immediate changes of the council related to the liturgy. However, there were also significant shifts in other dimensions of Catholic life.

"...for the first time in centuries, women were allowed to enter the sanctuary area and proclaim the word of God. Lay people were allowed to assist the priest in the distribution of communion and the Eucharist was now available 'under both species'. The host could now be received on the hand rather than the previous practice of receiving it on the tongue while kneeling."

Vatican II encouraged genuine ecumenical dialogue with non-Catholic Christians who were no longer called 'heretics' and 'schismatics' but 'separated brothers and sisters'. Gone was the painful prohibition on Catholics entering non-Catholic churches for weddings, baptisms and funerals, especially of extended family and friends. Catholics were encouraged to pray with other Christians and collaborate on social justice projects. In Australia this began the tradition of local joint ecumenical services around Pentecost Sunday, Advent Christmas carols, and the Good Friday walk of Stations of the Cross that visited Catholic, Anglican, Uniting and Baptist churches. Related to the renewal of the liturgy and ecumenical initiatives was the renewed appreciation of the word of God for Catholics who once considered matters relating to the Bible as something only Protestants did! Lay people were encouraged to study the scriptures and theology in a critical way. Theological colleges and institutes around Australia began to offer degrees in theology for laity as per the council's directives that such theological study was not a privilege granted, but a right bestowed by baptism. Theology was no longer 'secret men's business' confined to the hallowed halls of isolated seminaries. Lay women and religious undertook serious theological studies often in ecumenical institutes around Australia, known as colleges of divinity. Not only were they seated alongside future priests gaining the same degree in theology but many proceeded to postgraduate research with a masters or doctorate in theology, gaining a qualification and expertise far beyond what most priests achieved in the seminary. Within time, some of these women began to lecture in seminaries and theological colleges. This was simply inconceivable when the Council of Trent closed in 1563.

Cultural shifts of the 1960s

Vatican II deepened within Catholics a concern for social justice and an awareness of some of the tectonic cultural shifts of the 1960s. These shifts called for the Church to enter into some form of dialogue with the modern world. They included the changing place of women in society, greater urbanisation and educational opportunities, decolonisation, poverty and economic development, the threat of nuclear war, space exploration, and domestic inventions that greatly changed family life – the motor car, the television and the telephone. The 1960s also ushered in something unique to the post-war period; an emerging and distinctive youth culture that manifested itself not just in rock-and-roll music. It also manifested itself by challenging all forms of prevailing authority that were constantly questioned; parental, political and ecclesiastical. Performers such as Bob Dylan sang the anthem of the era; 'The Times They Are A-changing'. When one closely examines key sections of *Gaudium et Spes* relating to the Church's relationship with the modern world, it can be seen that the fathers of Vatican II also detected something of this cultural upheaval.

How a Council 'speaks'

The thing immediately noticeable about the documents of Vatican II is the language used by the council fathers. Most of the previous councils were summoned during a time of political turbulence and theological upheaval or heresy. To combat these controversial issues, previous councils almost always used harsh and condemnatory language in the form of a canon. Each canon reaffirmed Catholic belief and teaching and ended with the phrase *anathema sit*, or, 'let them be excluded'. It was very black-and-white. Vatican II, on the other hand, used a form of language that was more 'invitational'.

The council documents, while critical of some elements of modern life not in harmony with the Christian faith, used an altogether different approach in terms of seeking dialogue and mutuality. Distinguished American Jesuit historian, John O'Malley, speaks of the 'rhetoric' of Vatican II as a style of language that held up the Christian faith for admiration, praise and edification. For the first time in the history of the Church, a council took serious note of contemporary changes to society and culture. Vatican II acknowledged the truly global cultural transformations of the post-war era that also touched on matters of faith and Catholic life. No longer was the Church seen as aloof from history or as a type of 'perfect society'. Vatican II confronted the Church with the challenge intended by John XXIII; that the patrimony of faith needed to be expressed in the language of the contemporary era as a response to changing historical circumstances.

Vatican II resulted in considerable change for the Church, especially in its outward appearance, its relationship to the modern world and in the language of the documents. Unlike previous councils, Vatican II did not issue new dogmatic pronouncements regarding the central truths of the deposit of faith. So much of what we call 'change', especially in the area of liturgy, was in fact the retrieval of ancient practices that had fallen into disuse. For centuries, particularly after the Council of Trent, the Catholic Church appeared as a great bastion against modern progress, its language and practices appearing timeless and unchanging. And yet from the early days of the Gospel message of Jesus preached along the shores of the Sea of Galilee, the Church has constantly changed and adapted itself to new historical epochs. For example, the early councils debated at length the nature and identity of Jesus, especially in how we understand his human and divine natures. New words and theological concepts emerged because the Gospel message was carried from predominantly Jewish audiences into Greek-speaking territories greatly influenced by pagan philosophy. New questions were asked about faith and revelation as proclaimed by the early Church; wider cultural influences were shaping ecclesial life and practice. The same can be seen when the early church developed from the small house churches, as described in the Acts of the Apostles, into grander 'basilica' churches, which in Rome copied the style of major public and civic buildings. Vatican II was the first time that a council acknowledged the importance of wider cultural and historical factors and this shaped the council's agenda. The council fathers wished to deliberately enter into dialogue with the global cultural and historical shifts of the twentieth century. John XXIII, the historian-pope, asked the assembled bishops to be aware of these epochal shifts and to 'think big', as opposed to seeing Vatican II as a council only concerned with minor administrative and canonical revisions. The documents of Vatican II demonstrate extraordinary theological reach and global/historical considerations like no previous council.

Documents of Vatican II

In the course of its four-year meeting, Vatican II produced sixteen official documents which are the formal legacy of the council and an insight into the mind of the bishops. These had been condensed from the almost seventy preparatory documents or schemata that had been produced during the initial period of consultation. While the final voting patterns demonstrate an overwhelming level of support, on the floor of the council the issues were hammered out often during intense debate which spilled out into the public forum. John O'Malley calls Vatican II 'the biggest committee meeting in history' and, as such, the documents reveal many compromises and constant revisions by the various mixed commissions working behind the scenes. The documents are sometimes repetitive and uneven; they vary in quality and impact depending on the level of engagement of a particular issue at the time. At times, some aspects of the documents appear a little 'dated' as they address the specific historical period of the 1960s, however many parts are still remarkably prophetic and demonstrate the fairly radical thinking of the time.

While John XXIII convoked the council and presided at its first session in 1962, none of the sixteen documents were approved during this time. All sixteen documents were formally approved and promulgated by John XXIII's successor, Paul VI. Like all church documents, there is a certain hierarchy or order of importance in terms of their level of 'authority'. For example, Vatican II issued four Constitutions, nine Decrees and three Declarations which constitute the complete corpus of the council's teaching. This was done, however, with more authority given to the former such as the Constitutions as opposed to the latter documents. (One could use the analogy of gold, silver and bronze medals at the Olympics. They are all important medals, however, the former rank higher than the latter). The documents are summarised below in terms of this order, the name of the text in both English and Latin and the date each was approved.

Below: Pope John XXIII handing out medals to athletes at the Olympics

Dogmatic Constitution on the Church, *Lumen Gentium*, 21 November 1964

Lumen Gentium, the document on the Church, was a significant shift in terms of Catholic ecclesiology. Lumen Gentium recovered a more sacramental view of the Church describing her as 'a sign and instrument of communion

with God and the entire human race'. *Lumen Gentium* describes the Church as the whole People of God, a pilgrim people called to make known the gift of God's salvation in Christ. While the document reaffirms the indispensable role of the hierarchy, *Lumen Gentium* lessened the emphasis on the juridical and institutional dimensions in order to highlight the Church as that paschal mystery born from the side of the crucified Christ. Rather than beginning with the hierarchical order or the papacy, the episcopate and the ministerial priesthood, *Lumen Gentium* defined the Church as the whole People of God from which comes the indispensable hierarchical offices as divinely constituted.

Lumen Gentium highlights the unique and distinctive place of the laity in the Church by virtue of their baptism and stresses that lay people share in the Church's saving mission. (Such sentiments are repeated and elaborated further on in the specific decree on the Laity). *Lumen Gentium* speaks of 'the universal call to holiness' and the dignity of the laity who share in the universal priesthood of Christ. Prior to Vatican II, most Catholics thought of 'holiness' as belonging to the saints, the pope, bishops, priests and consecrated religious. Now the council insisted that holiness is a gift given to all, especially through baptism which is our first vocation, and the doorway to salvation and the life of grace. Prior to Vatican II, most Catholics associated the word 'vocation' with priests, brothers and religious sisters. Now the council insisted that all the faithful receive their first vocation in baptism. *Lumen Gentium* holds in high regard members of both non-Catholic denominations and non-Christian religions, stating that the mystery of God's salvific will is not unknown to those 'who seek God with a sincere heart'. This is a major turn-around from previous Catholic attitudes of hostility and negative language such as 'schismatics', 'heretics' and 'heathens'. (Vatican II also issued specific documents on ecumenism and non-Christian religions.)

Dogmatic Constitution on Divine Revelation, *Dei Verbum*, 18 November 1965

Dei Verbum reminded the Church that 'revelation' was not simply a series of static dogmatic teachings, but the revealing of God's salvific will in Christ. Revelation is about the person of Jesus Christ revealing God's saving love for the world and announcing the presence of God's kingdom as good news – a kingdom of justice, love and peace, where Jesus Christ 'is both the mediator and the sum total of revelation'.

Dei Verbum paid particular attention to, and elaborated on, the importance of the Word of God in the life of the Church. It recommended that the riches of the scriptures be opened up and made more widely available to the faithful. This was a significant shift for the Catholic Church given that the Bible was often the domain of clergy and theologians, and often associated with Protestant practice. Now Catholics were encouraged to take up the Bible, to study the scriptures and use them as a genuine source of prayer. Following the council, the Church introduced what we now know as the three-yearly cycle of lectionary readings to broaden the use of scripture in Catholic worship and sacramental life. Prior to the council, the same readings were used every Sunday, year after year. This new cycle called on priests to become more acquainted with this biblical richness and thus develop new skills in biblical interpretation and in homily delivery.

Dei Verbum also opened up for Catholics a better understanding of the Bible in terms of its 'literary forms'. While the Church teaches that all scripture is 'inspired', not everything in the Bible can be relied upon for facts and biographical history. However, building on decades of biblical research, the council affirmed that the truth of faith is often expressed in various types of historical writing, in prophetical and poetical texts and in other forms of literary expression. For example, the four Gospels were written at different times, by different authors, for different audiences, each seeking to highlight particular themes of the earthly ministry of Jesus. The Gospels were not written chronologically as they appear in the Bible and are not complete 'biographies' of Jesus. Like all the documents of Vatican II, *Dei Verbum* uses uplifting and persuasive language to communicate the truths of faith in terms of the council's express wish that 'it wants the whole world to hear the summons to salvation, so that through hearing it may believe, through belief it may hope and through hope it may come to love'.

Constitution on the Sacred Liturgy, *Sacrosanctum Concilium*, 4 December 1963

This was the first document debated by the council and the one that had most immediate impact on Catholics and parish life at the local level. It was the liturgy in particular where Catholics became aware that major changes discussed in Rome would have significant impact on how they experienced the liturgy. For decades prior to Vatican II, liturgical scholars had been studying issues to do with the increased participation of the faithful, greater accessibility to the liturgical mysteries of the Church and the possibility of dialogue in the liturgy between the priest and the congregation.

This was a major shift in Catholic liturgical consciousness. For decades Catholics had been obliged to attend Mass or to 'hear' the Mass with many either saying the Rosary or following the liturgy in their missal. Now the council was insisting that 'the faithful should be led to take that full, conscious and active part in liturgical celebrations which is demanded by the nature of the liturgy itself'. The council also insisted on the liturgical principle that all the sacraments flow from the paschal mystery of Christ, that is his life, death and resurrection.

Pastoral Constitution on the Church in the Modern World, *Gaudium et Spes*, 7 December 1965

This was a truly remarkable and historic document of Vatican II. Unlike the other documents that had their genesis in some form of preparatory schemata, *Gaudium et Spes* was literally born on the floor of the council and was part of the express desire of the bishops to say something about the Church's relationship to the world. In previous eras, the Church had an often antagonistic attitude to 'the world' and typically condemned numerous advances or developments such as democracy, scientific discovery, new insights into sociology and anthropology, freedom of conscience and freedom of the press. The bishops at Vatican II, inspired by John XXIII, wanted to enter into some form of positive dialogue with the world and the rapid changes of the twentieth century in order to better assist the Church in its saving mission.

Gaudium et Spes is remarkable in its length and breadth. Whereas the other documents

speak specifically on religious and ecclesial matters such as the priesthood, religious life, the liturgy and divine revelation, *Gaudium et Spes* covers issues not normally associated with conciliar documents. For example, it deals with the rapid changes in history following the Second World War, urbanisation, industrialisation, human rights, social justice, world poverty, war and nuclear threat, marriage and the family, conscience and international relations. Never before had a council of the Church so consciously addressed strictly worldly and secular issues in both a positive light and in relationship to matters of faith in terms of the Church's mission. There is no doubt that *Gaudium et Spes* had its genesis in the positive and universal pastoral outlook of John XXIII, so beautifully expressed in his opening speech on 11 October 1962. Far from being antagonistic to modern developments, John XXIII wanted the council to interpret these changes and to engage with the world in order to enhance the Church's proclamation of the Gospel.

Gaudium et Spes is remembered by many for its prophetic opening statement:

> The joys and hopes, the griefs and anguish of the people of our time, especially of those who are poor or afflicted, are the joys and hopes, the grief and anguish of the followers of Christ as well.

Five decades after the council, the Church is called to go deeper into this document and to draw forth prophetic insights in terms of the call to human solidarity and a renewed sense of mission:

> In every age, the Church carries the responsibility of reading the signs of the times and of interpreting them in the light of the Gospel, if it is to carry out its task ...We must be aware of and understand the aspirations, the yearnings, and often the dramatic features of the world in which we live ... Ours is a new age of history with profound and rapid changes spreading gradually to all corners of the earth ...We are entitled then to speak of a real social and cultural transformation whose repercussions are felt at the religious level also.

While this document was addressed to the rapidly changing world of the 1960s, it is equally relevant and appropriate for our own time. These sentiments of *Gaudium et Spes* were not entirely new for the Church; they reflect the growing body of Catholic social teaching that emerged in 1891 with Pope Leo XIII's landmark encyclical on the industrial revolution, *Rerum Novarum*. In 1891 Leo XIII recognised in a subtle way how the dramatic changes to the working conditions of life also had implications and consequences for urban, parish and family life. In *Gaudium et Spes*, the Church acknowledged this more explicitly in terms of wanting to enter into dialogue with the truly global changes of the time.

Decree on the Instruments of Social Communication, *Inter Mirifica*, 4 December 1963

This decree on mass media is perhaps the weakest of all the council's documents. It was written in the context of the television technology which was relatively new in the 1960s and the increasing influence of media in urban life. On the whole, the bishops endorsed this as a sign of progress in modern society and expressed caution over certain types of media that may be morally harmful, especially to the young. The council encouraged priests and laity to understand the media and to use it effectively in the proclamation of the Gospel and for other forms of pastoral engagement. The bishops encouraged the establishment of national offices to coordinate the work of the Catholic press, cinema, radio and television and for laity to be suitably qualified to undertake this work.

Naturally the council could not have predicted the rapid development of media technology that we have witnessed in recent years, especially the revolution of social media that has completely transformed our lives. Social analysts speak of how the digital world has completely changed the way news and information is constructed, accessed and disseminated. Traditional forms of media are fast disappearing and young people in particular use social media in vastly different ways to not only organise their lives, but also to understand their place in the world.

Decree on Ecumenism, *Unitatis Redintegratio*, 21 November 1964

The decree on Ecumenism reflects much of the spirit of John XXIII's specific call that Vatican II seek the path of Christian unity. For decades prior to the council, the Catholic Church's limited understanding of ecumenism was for 'a return to Rome', especially of those denominations that had been formed in the wake of the Protestant Reformation. The use of such terms as 'schismatics' and 'dissidents' were not exactly conducive to warm ecumenical dialogue! Now the council placed ecumenism as a central concern for the Church. Catholics who lived before Vatican II recall, with some pain, the prohibition on attending baptisms, funerals and weddings of relatives and friends in non-Catholic churches. Catholics marrying non-Catholics could not celebrate the wedding in the main body of the church but had a shortened ceremony performed in the sacristy where the priest would vest for Mass. In the wake of the council, all this changed.

As a result of Vatican II, ecumenical dialogue now occurs at the highest international and national level, and involves bishops and theologians reflecting together, praying together and discussing many contested areas of theology. At the local level Christians pray together, share worship, study the Bible together, participate in ecumenical activities such as social justice projects, and walk in witness during the Stations of the Cross on Good Friday. Over the years, in parishes across Australia, local groups of pastors, ministers and vicars would form a 'ministers fraternal' in order to pray, share a meal and plan joint activities. Across rural and regional Australia, denominations sometimes share the same building for Sunday worship and some dioceses have signed formal 'covenants' that bind church bodies to regular worship and action together. One of the major developments since Vatican II has been the development of interfaith initiatives especially in the major capital cities. Diocesan ecumenical offices now incorporate formal interfaith links with Muslim, Jewish, Hindu and Buddhist communities.

Ecumenism since Vatican II has made progress slowly. During the optimism of the 1960s, many thought that historical obstacles could simply be removed and Christian unity achieved. However, major stumbling blocks remain. While many Catholics feel a sense of closeness to Anglicans and the traditions that emerged after the Reformation, there is still less than full agreement on issues regarding the sacraments and the nature of ordained ministry. On the other hand, the Catholic Church, while recognising the validity of the sacraments of the Eastern orthodox tradition, still cannot come to agreement on issues regarding jurisdiction and papal primacy.

Decree on the Catholic Eastern Churches, *Orientalium Ecclesiarum*, 21 November 1964

This relatively short decree concerns those distinct eastern Churches that while retaining their unique liturgical, theological, spiritual and canonical traditions, are in fact in full communion with the Holy See. These traditions include Coptic, Chaldean, Maronite, Melkite, Assyrian, Ukrainian and Syro-Malabar Catholics. While the majority of Catholics around the world belong to the Roman or Latin-rite tradition, these Churches of ancient origin, particularly around the Middle East, have distinctive forms of liturgy, governance and spirituality.

In a country such as Australia, these communities are quite numerous and it is not uncommon for children of these traditions to attend local Catholic primary schools. Occasionally, Latin-rite Catholics attend ceremonies in some of these churches and may come

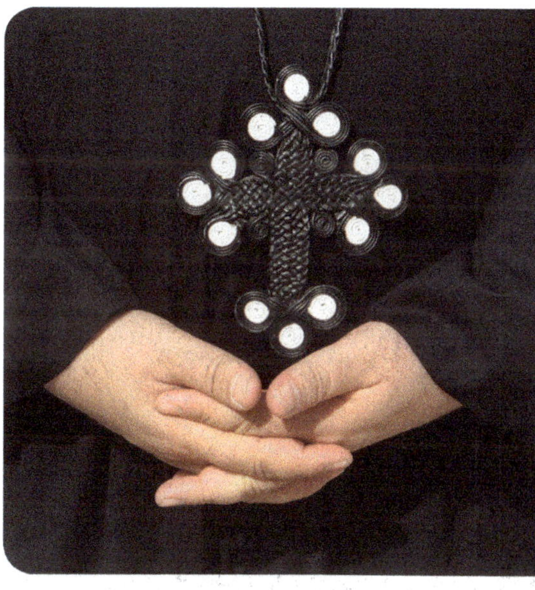

away with a mistaken notion that they have attended an 'orthodox' ceremony of another denomination without realising that they have participated in a tradition fully in communion with Rome. Vatican II affirmed that these churches or traditions are never to be seen as some form of 'inferior' Catholicism and, in fact, are to be esteemed and held in high regard. The grand entrance procession into St Peter's Basilica at the commencement of Vatican II demonstrated this diversity and universality in terms of quite distinctive episcopal garments that broke the monotony of the waves of white-mitred, Latin-rite bishops.

Decree on the Pastoral Office of Bishops in the Church, *Christus Dominus*, 28 October 1965

It is no accident that the word 'pastoral' is inserted in the title of this document, as indeed it could have been for every document of Vatican II, given John XXIII's express wish that the council would have an overall pastoral orientation. It was John XXIII's emphasis of his role as pastor and shepherd of the universal Church that underlies *Christus Dominus.* For centuries, popes and bishops both acted and looked like worldly monarchs and feudal lords. John XXIII shifted the emphasis and his style recovered a servant-model of Gospel inspired leadership, a more biblical emphasis of pope and bishop acting as genuine pastors and shepherds not only of their Catholic flock, but also with a pastoral concern for all believers and those with no discernible faith whatsoever.

Christus Dominus recovered the notion of collegiality in the Church. While the pope is ultimately the head of the Catholic Church and the final source of appeal, all the bishops of the world share with him in the governance of the Church. As a body, the bishops form a college of authority 'with Peter and under Peter' and the council itself was the concrete embodiment of collegiality at work. An extension of this principle was the formation of the Synod of Bishops in the wake of Vatican II, a regular meeting of a representative group of Catholic bishops from around the world with the pope to consider particular aspects of the Church's mission. Since Vatican II, such synods have gathered normally every three years to either discuss a particular topic such as the family, religious life or laity, or to look at the Church in a particular geographical area such as Asia, Africa or the Middle East.

Another significant aspect of *Christus Dominus* is the way it positioned the diocesan bishop as the leader of the local church in communion with the Bishop of Rome, and not as some form of junior branch manager of a multinational organisation. By virtue of their consecration, bishops are successors of the apostles and diocesan bishops in particular make present the mystery of the universal Church in a particular geographical area. They are called to be the leaders, teachers, pastors and sources of ecclesial unity for that particular diocese.

Decree on Priestly Formation, *Optatum Totius*, 28 October 1965

This decree contains one of the most repeated phrases of Vatican II, 'adaptation to the new and changing conditions of modern life'. It is implied in this decree that priestly formation could no longer be undertaken in a vacuum or in some form of monastic seclusion from the world. Future priests are to be trained in the various theological disciplines in order to be formed as teachers and shepherds. However, they are to also take account of intellectual and cultural trends in their own particular region of the world so as to better proclaim the Gospel and 'enter into dialogue with the people of their time'. Priests are called to work collaboratively with the lay faithful.

The document also discusses the importance of integrating human insights and modern psychology into seminary formation. This decree is closely related to the following one which treats in a much more comprehensive way the ministry and life of priests.

Decree on the Ministry and Life of Priests, *Presbyterorum Ordinis*, 7 December 1965

This decree is much more explicit in terms of helping priests to be aware of the many new challenges that would face them in their daily ministry. The council's reappraisal of the place of the Word of God in the life of the Church demands of priests not only a better understanding of the scriptures, but also a consideration of the changed social/cultural context of their preaching. What the council decreed in 1965 is just as important and relevant for

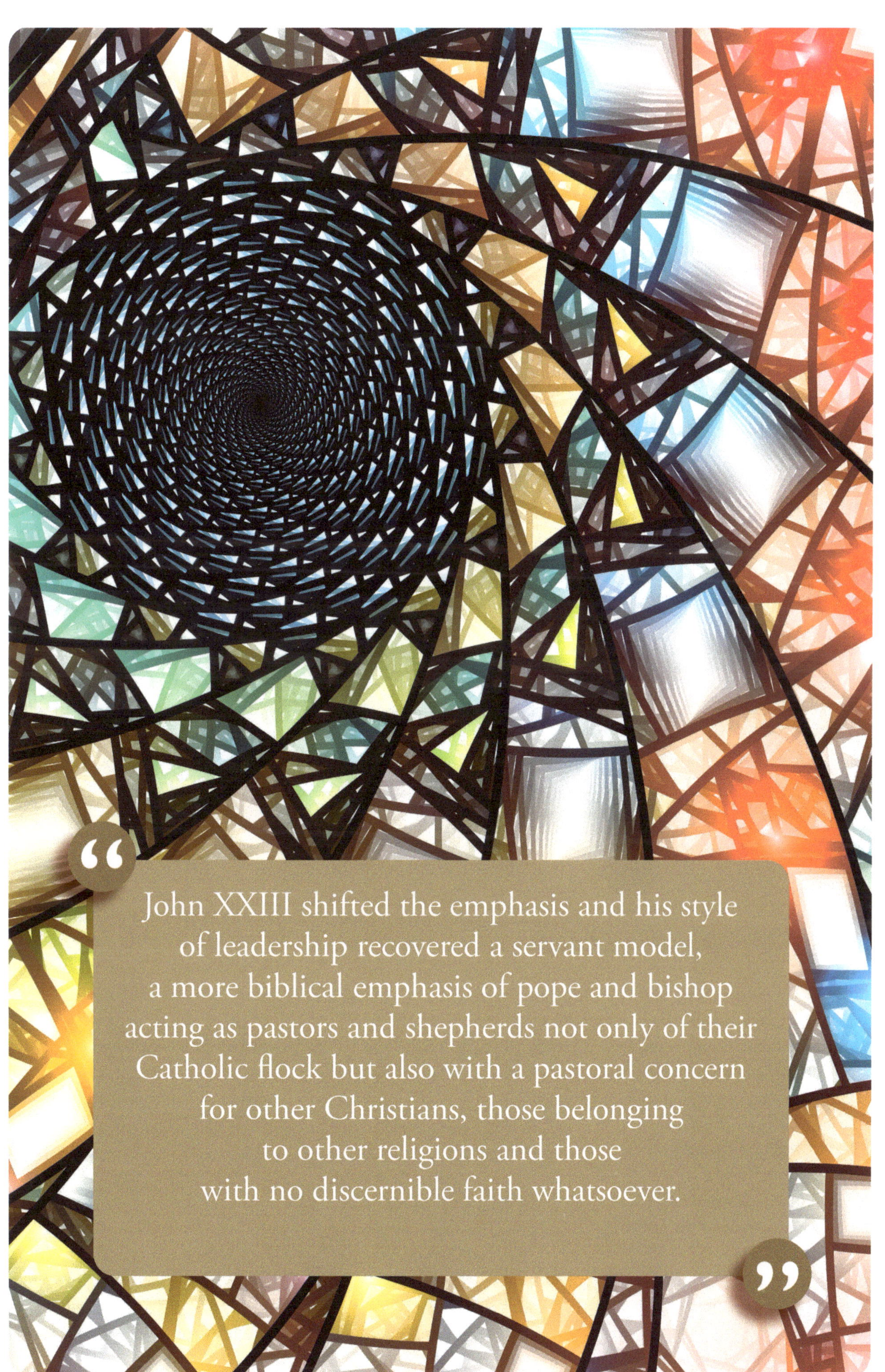

“John XXIII shifted the emphasis and his style of leadership recovered a servant model, a more biblical emphasis of pope and bishop acting as pastors and shepherds not only of their Catholic flock but also with a pastoral concern for other Christians, those belonging to other religions and those with no discernible faith whatsoever.”

the contemporary Church:

> Moreover, the priest's preaching, often very difficult in present-day circumstances, if it is to become effective in moving the minds of his hearers, must expound the word of God not merely in a general and abstract way but by the application of the eternal truth of the Gospel to the concrete circumstances of life.

Priests are reminded that they share a sacramental bond with each other and with their bishop, acting as 'co-workers' with the bishop in proclaiming the good news. Hence Vatican II directed that each diocese was to have a senate or council of priests whom the bishop would consult in assisting his leadership and in planning appropriate pastoral strategies. Priests are called to work collaboratively with lay people 'and to break new ground in pastoral methods under the guidance of the Spirit'. In Australia, this directive of the council is seen most clearly in pastoral leadership teams, especially in the employment of pastoral workers and a range of faith formators in parishes. Priestly leadership no longer means simply being the 'boss' and shouting orders to those under him. Genuine priestly leadership now involves calling forward the skills and charisms of lay people, especially in the administration of large and complex parish entities, and working collaboratively with a shared sense of mission.

Decree on the Up-To-Date Renewal of Religious Life, *Perfectae Caritatis*, 28 October 1965

The most salient feature of this decree was the call for all religious men and women to 'go back' to their roots and the original inspiration of their respective founders. This was in order to renew religious life so as to 'adapt to the changed conditions of life and evaluate the contemporary world wisely in the light of faith'. The themes of renewal and adaptation are very strong in this document. Religious orders, congregations and institutes that were founded centuries ago were called upon by the council to renew their customs, traditions, constitutions and missionary apostolates in order to adapt to the new demands of their respective ministries.

The most radical form of this renewal began with religious dress. Nuns with long flowing habits and faces almost totally covered adopted a more modern form of religious dress, often suited to the climatic conditions of their location. Religious sisters discovered that the original 'charism' of their founder required of them not to be locked up behind high convent walls but to minister to the poor and marginalised of their day. Women and men religious, especially those in teaching orders, were given much more freedom to study at secular universities and to branch out into new ministries beyond Catholic schools, hospitals and orphanages. Interestingly, this decree of Vatican II did not repeat the teaching of the Council of Trent which stated that religious life was a 'superior' state to married life.

Decree on the Apostolate of the Laity, *Apostolicam Actuositatem*, 18 November 1965

This is the document that was perhaps Vatican II's finest hour. Previous council documents were generally addressed to bishops, priests, religious and theologians. Here Vatican II had something specific, powerful and prophetic to say to the laity of the Church. The laity are recognised for their unique and distinctive place in the life of the Church by virtue of their baptism and their universal call to holiness. The laity share in the universal mission of the Church in their own right and not simply as 'helpers' of the clergy. They are called to live their vocation of witness and service 'in the world' and to transform the world by their proclamation of the Gospel. This decree builds on the particular force given to the lay vocation in *Lumen Gentium* and is the result of a specific theology of the laity. This theology had been developed in the Church through Catholic Action and the work of outstanding leaders like Rosemary Goldie and theologians such as the Dominican Yves Congar. As a result of the council, new opportunities began to open up for lay people in terms of studying theology, scripture and liturgy and taking up senior positions of leadership in Church administration. Mistakenly at times, these senior roles that lay people occupy in Church administration, theological institutes and diocesan agencies are seen as a substitute when most of these roles were once occupied by clerics. But a more mature vision of the council is that these roles are now occupied by those whose gifts and charisms are essential and unique to the life of the Church and never because of a relative shortage of priests.

Decree of the Church's Missionary Activity, *Ad Gentes*, 7 December 1965

This decree expresses a shift in attitude in terms of the Church's missionary activity. Whereas in previous centuries some Church officials felt they were evangelising and bringing western culture to missionary outposts, Vatican II affirmed that the proclamation of the Gospel had to be sensitive to local conditions. More importantly, the council recommended the adaptation of catechesis in order for it to be in harmony with the character of the local people. Here the council promoted the idea of dialogue and moves away from various forms of European cultural superiority. It stated that the richness and beauty of the Gospel is to enter into a respectful dialogue with the people and customs of the various parts of the world where the Church's missionary efforts occur.

The decree is a reminder that the Church is essentially missionary by its very nature. The document hints at the fact that many countries at that time were beginning to throw off the yoke of western colonialism and seek their own rightful independence in the international community. This was especially the case in Africa and Asia and the council encouraged all missionaries to be aware of such circumstances:

> They must approach people with an open mind and heart ... and generously accommodate themselves to the different customs and changing circumstances of other peoples.

Declaration on Christian Education, *Gravissimum Educationis*, 28 October 1965

This is perhaps not the strongest document issued by the council. Other than reminding parents that they are the first educators of their children, the document does not have a coherent framework and seems to focus on making general points about Catholic schools and universities. As is often the case, the council hints at the changing sphere of education in general and how technology and systems of thought will inevitably change the way people learn and engage with culture.

In many parts of the world, the greatest change in Catholic education saw a significant increase in the number of qualified lay teachers now working in schools that once were administered exclusively by women and men religious. This was certainly the case in Australia and radically changed the make-up of these schools.

Declaration on the Relationship of the Church to Non-Christian Religions, *Nostra Aetate*, 28 October 1965

While this document is in the lowest category of council authority, it generated much intense debate. It began as a statement of the Church's relationship to the Jewish people but was expanded to include people of various religions around the world. The council stated that there are elements of 'truth' in these quite diverse religions and that God's love is never denied to those who seek him with a sincere heart. This was a significant shift for the Church from before the council proudly proclaiming 'no salvation outside the Church' to now saying that 'the Catholic Church rejects nothing of what is true and holy in these religions'.

The issue of the Church's relationship to the Jewish people was a 'hot-button' issue at Vatican II, especially after Pius XII's alleged 'silence' in the wake of the Holocaust. The Church rejected any form of discrimination or persecution of the Jewish people. The council also rejected the notion of 'deicide', that is, that the Jewish people as a race were responsible for the crucifixion of Jesus. (When John XXIII was a papal diplomat in Turkey and Greece during the Second World War, he issued false baptism certificates to Jewish people to save them from the gas chambers. As pope, he once was travelling through Rome in his open-top vehicle which passed a local synagogue with people spilling out. He stood up and removed his skullcap as a sign of respect. The Jewish people never forgot such gestures).

Declaration on Religious Liberty, *Dignitatis Humanae*, 7 December 1965

Like the previous document, this one on religious freedom caused intense debate on the floor of the council because it appeared to be upturning a previously held teaching 'that error has no rights'. While claiming the right of religious freedom, the Church affirms that an individual can never be 'compelled' to believe and that, by definition, faith is a person's free response to God's gift and grace.

Given the acute climate of the awareness and promotion of human rights, the document states: 'People nowadays are becoming increasingly conscious of the dignity of the human person ... This Vatican council pays careful attention to these spiritual aspirations ...' According to the council, the right to religious freedom is based on the very dignity of the human person. This was a significant development of doctrine for the Church and led some to erroneously believe that the truth of the Gospel was somewhat compromised if human beings exercised their freedom to reject it.

Understanding the Council that changed our lives

It is now over five decades since the close of Vatican II. The council was convoked by John XXIII, a much loved and admired pope, in order for the Church to renew its mission and engage in a more fruitful and pastoral dialogue with the modern world. The documents of Vatican II speak in a unique way, unlike previous councils which issued canons and condemnations (*anathema sit:* 'let them be excluded'). While there was intense debate on the council floor, the final documents were approved by an overwhelming majority by the voting bishops. As the documents were released, studied and implemented, there appeared the first signs of tension between the 'letter' of the council (that which is contained in the documents) and the 'spirit' of the council, a more pastoral, open-minded and bridge-building attitude that went beyond the written word.

Paul VI made dialogue the centrepiece of his papacy. But he also used his papal authority to remove controversial issues from conciliar debate. These issues included priestly celibacy and birth control, and his right to reserve for himself the task of implementing the Synod of Bishops. Following the council, many thought that the Church would shift on mandatory celibacy. It did not. As the papal commission on birth control continued its deliberations, expectations were high that the Church might change its position on artificial birth control. It did not. In 1968, Paul VI issued the encyclical *Humanae Vitae* which reiterated Catholic teaching on this issue. There was immense fallout. Priests and religious resigned en masse from the Church. Many lay people expressed public disagreement. The Church was criticised, with many challenging papal authority.

All these factors added to the climate of 'crisis' in this period. 1968 was the year of university riots and uprisings around the world. Politically enlightened student activists challenged the authority of parents, politicians, university professors and the Church. Joseph Ratzinger, the young German theology professor and *peritus* (theological adviser) at Vatican II, was deeply shocked when students took over lecture theatres. The sexual revolution was dramatically unfolding together with feminism, civil rights and marches against the Vietnam War. The dialogue and pastoral outreach of Vatican II seemed to collide with the cultural turmoil and upheavals of the 1960s.

Within the Church, papal authority was often challenged. At times, Paul VI appeared as a pontiff under siege, caught between the more progressive voices in the Church sometimes clashing with more conservative attitudes. During the council there was disagreement but by the 1960s and 1970s there was open defiance. Some had felt that the council had gone too far and embraced the values of the modern world; others felt that the Church needed to make more progress.

Joseph Ratzinger continued to have reservations about some aspects of Vatican II renewal. In 1981, Cardinal Ratzinger became the head of the Congregation for the Doctrine of the Faith and shared these reservations with Pope John Paul II (1978-2005) who called him to Rome. Karol Wojtyla was a young bishop at Vatican II and contributed to the document *Gaudium et Spes*. Both men were seen as putting the 'brakes' on conciliar renewal and expressed their concern that groundbreaking documents like *Gaudium et Spes* were a little too optimistic about the human condition and the place of dialogue between the Church and the world. John Paul II was an extraordinary global pastor and missionary, visiting parts of the world where a pope had never been. However, he always maintained firm papal teaching.

Pope Benedict XVI

When John Paul II died in 2005, he was succeeded by Ratzinger who took the name Benedict XVI. He used the papal office to repeat his concerns from the 1960s. Ratzinger believed that in the enthusiasm for Vatican II renewal, a culture had been created in the Church whereby everything before the council had to be figuratively consigned to history, and a new 'church' had to created.

Ratzinger's election in 2005 coincided with the fortieth anniversary of Vatican II's conclusion in 1965. In the traditional end-of-year address to the Roman Curia, the pope noted this historic coincidence and stated:

> ... it all depends on the correct interpretation of the council or – as we would say today – on its proper hermeneutics, the correct key to its interpretation and application. The problems in its implementation arose from the fact that two contrary hermeneutics came face-to-face and quarrelled with each other. One caused confusion, the other, silently but more and more visibly, bore and is bearing fruit.
>
> On the one hand, there is an interpretation that I would call 'a hermeneutic of discontinuity and rupture'; it has frequently availed itself of the sympathies of the mass media, and also one trend of modern theology. On the other, there is the 'hermeneutic of reform', of renewal in the continuity of the one-subject Church that the Lord has given to us. She is a subject that increases in time and develops; yet always remaining the same, the one subject of the journeying People of God (M. Lamb & M. Levering, *Vatican II: Renewal within Tradition*, Oxford University Press, 2008, pp. ix-xv.)

Benedict XVI was very subtle here in affirming that in the wake of Vatican II there was reform and renewal in the Church, that is, some form of change. However, in his mind, it was not the form of change championed by Vatican II enthusiasts by which the Church was literally turned upside-down. Benedict XVI affirms a type of slow, gentle and organic form of change in the Church. The latter part of this quote is almost verbatim from the words of the now canonised St John Henry Newman (1801-1890) in his seminal 1845 work, *The Development of Christian Doctrine*.

Some felt that Benedict XVI's 2005 address was a direct rebuttal of a particular form of historical scholarship on Vatican II that emanated from the 'Bologna school' in northern Italy. This 'school' has been considered to have been started when the John XXIII Foundation was co-founded in the 1950s by the Italian historian Giuseppe Alberigo (1926-2007) and the then archbishop of Bologna and leading figure at Vatican II, Cardinal Giacomo Lercaro (1891-1976). Between 1995 and 2006, Alberigo and his colleagues published a magisterial five-volume international work called *The History of Vatican II*. It highlighted Vatican II as an epochal, global event for the Church and promoted a much more progressive interpretation of the council, as opposed to a more traditional interpretation of the council based solely on the texts alone. All historians and theologians affirm that Vatican II remained in continuity with the ancient deposit of faith (as emphasised by Benedict XVI). However, the nature of change in the wake of the council was such that it was no longer 'business as usual' for the Church. Vatican II brought about a significant shift in language, customs and practices while remaining in fundamental 'continuity' with tradition.

Below: Pope Francis and Pope Benedict XVI at the canonisation of Saints John XXIII and John Paul II at St Peter's Square in Rome

The Nature of Change

As mentioned earlier, the first document debated by the bishops and the first area of change was the liturgy. The Latin liturgy that previous generations had grown up with had remained largely unchanged since the close of the Council of Trent in 1563. The changes at Vatican II were 'revolutionary' in the eyes of many and appeared to up-end centuries of practice. However, a close reading of history reveals that many liturgical reforms introduced at Vatican II were not new or revolutionary but in fact the retrieval of earlier customs that had fallen into disuse. Speaking in the vernacular (not Latin), communion on the hand, communion from the chalice, the priest facing the people, the removal of altar rails – these were all practices re-introduced by Vatican II. While on the surface they appeared as novel, these changes are evidence of decades of liturgical scholarship and development.

It was Pope St Pius X (1903-1914), hardly a revolutionary, who lowered the age for the reception of First Communion and encouraged frequent, even daily reception of the Eucharist by the faithful. With his reform of church music, Pius X encouraged liturgical 'participation' and 'accessibility' by the faithful. In the 1950s, Pius XII (1939-1958) simplified the Holy Week ceremonies and restored the Easter Vigil from a morning celebration (in daylight) to its proper evening setting. He also authorised some evening Masses, partial use of the vernacular and a relaxation of the eucharistic fast.

As John O'Malley points out, one of the difficulties of reading the Vatican II documents is that the council, by its very nature, was to be the guardian of the Church's patrimony of faith. Unlike previous councils, Vatican II defined no new dogma or teaching or changed any of the central tenets of faith defined in the Creed. But by using a new form of language or 'rhetoric', the council did make major changes in the life of the Church. Vatican II did not 'change' the Church as such, but did set the Church in a new direction. But nowhere in the documents is this stated explicitly.

For example, you arrive at the train station expecting to go to destination X. Suddenly an announcement is made: 'Passengers please note. The train on platform 1 is not going to destination X but destination Y'. You now know that the train is going in another direction. It has been *explicitly* stated. But this was not the case at Vatican II. Changes were made without explicit acknowledgement. In fact, ambiguities emerged in areas such as the liturgy. For example, *Sacrosanctum Concilium* states 'The use of the Latin language ... is to be preserved in the Latin rites'(no. 36.1). 'But since the use of the vernacular ... may frequently be of great advantage to the people, a wider use may be made of it ...' (36.2). And further along, the document states, 'Even in the liturgy the church does not wish to impose a rigid uniformity in matters which do not affect the faith or wellbeing of the entire community. Rather does it cultivate and foster the qualities and talents of the various races and nations' (37). So there will be Latin and, on the other hand, there won't be Latin!

Another example was the council's positive attitude to the world in *Gaudium et Spes*. For centuries popes had denounced freedom of conscience, freedom of religion, freedom of the press and the separation of church and state. This made sense in the wake of the French Revolution (1799) and the loss of the Papal States (1870). Vatican II adopted a more nuanced perspective and chose the language of mutuality,

dialogue, brotherhood and working for the common good. Non-Catholics were no longer castigated for being 'heretics' and 'schismatics'. A change in attitude, language and direction was evident but none of the documents announce explicitly, like the train station analogy, 'Attention passengers; this train is now departing for another destination'. The council, in an authoritative way, reinterpreted centuries of antagonistic teaching against the world without explicitly saying as much but doing so in the light of the new needs of the time.

The documents of Vatican II need to be held in tension and interpreted in context. The best context is to return to John XXIII's opening speech on 11 October 1962. At no stage in that speech did John XXIII state what Benedict XVI feared the most – that there would be a demolition of the ancient ecclesial reality and the construction of a new type of 'church' more in conformity with the modern age. John XXIII stated that he wanted to change not so much the ancient 'deposit of faith', but the way the Church went about proclaiming its message by adapting itself to the new historical circumstances of the twentieth century:

> I confidently trust that under the light of this council the Church will become richer in spiritual matters and, with this new energy, will look to the future without fear. In fact, by bringing itself up-to-date where needed, the Church will make people, families and whole nations really turn their minds toward divine things …
>
> In fact, at the present time, Divine Providence is leading us to a new order of human relations which, by the very effort of the people of this time, is directed toward the fulfilment of God's great plan for us. Everything, even human differences, leads to greater good for the Church …
>
> Here is a key distinction on which our work is based: The substance of our central beliefs is one thing, and the way it is presented is another. It is this latter presentation of the faith with which we are concerned here, and our approach to this will be a thoroughly pastoral one (B. Huebsch, *Vatican II in Plain English: The Council*, Vol. I, Thomas More Publishing, Allen: Texas, 1996, pp. 85-95.)

In the years after the council, the nature of the many changes instituted by Vatican II continued to be debated, especially to the extent that they were faithful to this vision of legitimate adaptation outlined by John XXIII. Twenty years after the close of Vatican II, in 1985 John Paul II called an Extraordinary Synod of Bishops to commemorate and reflect on the council. The pope praised the council's achievements but ensured that further developments would be made under tight papal supervision. In the shadows, Cardinal Ratzinger maintained the importance of fidelity to the 'text' of the council's documents as opposed to excessive enthusiasm for the council's 'spirit'. Ratzinger maintained this focus when he succeeded John Paul II. However, in 2013 Benedict XVI did make a decision of enormous historical significance. He resigned the papacy.

Pope John Paul II at Lone Pine Koala Sanctuary, Australia, 1986

> John XXIII stated that he wanted to change not so much the ancient 'deposit of faith', but the way the Church went about proclaiming its message by adapting itself to the new historical circumstances of the twentieth century.

Chapter 4

Pope Francis: Living the Spirit and Grace of the Council

In 2013 it did not appear that the eighty-six-year-old Benedict XVI would be making any radical decisions. In public he began to look frail but his sharp mind was as lucid as ever. The papacy took him to distant countries and such journeys took a considerable toll on him. Power disputes in the curia and the release of sensitive Vatican information gave the impression that the burdens of office and the demands of the modern papacy were too much for a man of advanced years. The possibility of a papal 'resignation' was discussed openly during the final years of John Paul II's reign when serious illness had limited his speech and mobility. With the benefit of hindsight, historians now look back to the 'clue' that Benedict XVI gave about the possibility of a papal resignation. In 2009, he made an official visit to the town of L'Aquila in the Abruzzo region that had been devastated by an earthquake. The basilica of the city holds the tomb of Celestine V who resigned the papacy in 1294 after only five months and retired to the monastic life. On this visit in 2009, Benedict XVI removed his papal pallium and placed it on the tomb of Celestine V.

Monday 11 February 2013 appeared to be a normal day in the Vatican. The pope delivered a speech announcing a group of new saints to be canonised. Towards the end of the speech he made a startling announcement. In clear and precise Latin, calmly and without fanfare, Benedict XVI stated that he had examined his conscience before God and he had come to the certainty that his advanced age was no longer suited to the exercise of the Petrine ministry. He would freely renounce his ministry as Bishop of Rome and the See of Rome would be vacant on 28 February 2013. It was a bombshell announcement of historic proportions, more dramatic than the announcement of a council in 1959 by John XXIII.

On 13 March 2013, the Argentine cardinal Jorge Mario Bergoglio was elected to the papacy. He was a rank outsider, but some may remember that his name appeared in the 2005 conclave that had elected Ratzinger to the papacy. It would be a papacy of many 'firsts'. Bergoglio was the first Jesuit in history, the first from Latin America, and the first to take the name of the revered saint from Assisi, Francis. Bergoglio's simplicity of life known from his days in Buenos Aires would be carried into the papacy. Francis came from a humble working-class family from northern Italy who had immigrated to Argentina. His time as head of the Jesuits in Argentina was controversial but as an auxiliary bishop, archbishop and cardinal, he was known for travelling on the metro to visit outlying parishes, as well as for living in a modest apartment, not an episcopal mansion.

Pope Francis – a theologian of the streets

Just as John XXIII shocked many by his warm, humble and engaging style of ministry in 1958, Pope Francis did the same. Francis insisted on much less formality from his first day in office. He returned to the international hotel for priests in Rome where he had always stayed to collect his belongings, pay his account and thank the staff personally. He eschewed the papal limousine in order to travel in the bus with the cardinals that had just elected him. Having taken the name of the great saint from Assisi, Pope Francis chose not to live in the Apostolic Palace, insisting that he would live instead in Casa Santa Marta, the communal residence adjacent to St Peter's for priests and bishops working in the Vatican. The pope has two simple rooms and takes his meals with others in the communal dining room. Francis celebrates Mass not on his own but with a regular congregation in the chapel of Santa Marta. He models Gospel simplicity and servant leadership. He is the first pope to come from a religious order since the election of the Camaldolese monk, Gregory XVI, in 1831.

In his first homilies and addresses, Pope Francis demonstrated a particular concern for the poor, the broken and the marginalised. During his numerous pastoral visits in Buenos Aires he saw grinding poverty, shanty towns and crime, but was always moved by the faith and devotion of the faithful. Francis is a theologian of the streets, a Jesuit 'contemplative in action'. Like John XXIII, he teaches not with learned theological texts but by powerful gestures and direct speech. In one address, Pope Francis lamented the 'culture of waste' in modern society and insisted that when we throw out food, 'we are taking it from the tables of the poor'. He is constantly admonishing priests and bishops that they are to be close to their people, to have 'the smell of the sheep'. He rails against clericalism, privilege and entitlement insisting that priests and bishops are called to humbly live the Gospel, not to advance their careers and seek promotion in the Church. No one 'handles' Pope Francis; there is no papal court of attendants. He carries his own bag, wears his own shoes (not pontifical slippers) and dons a simple pectoral cross with simple vestments.

A missionary Church

He speaks about a missionary Church at 'the peripheries', a Church of close pastoral encounter that binds up the physical, spiritual and moral wounds of daily existence. For him, the power of the Gospel is not at the 'centre' of ecclesiastical power but at the 'peripheries' which he knows a great deal about. His most dramatic gestures in this regard concern his nomination of cardinals from around the world. Pope Francis nominates cardinals not from 'traditional' sees and large metropolitan cities that are automatically given the red hat, but from obscure and far-flung places from around the world that have never had a resident cardinal. He nominates cardinals in places such as Tonga, Papua New Guinea, Bangladesh, Mauritius, the Central African Republic, Cape Verde and Morocco. He downplays the role of cardinals as 'princes' of the Church with all the glittering honour and privilege that was once associated with this office.

Below: Pope Francis takes part in the historic canonisation of Popes John XXIII and John Paul II at St Peter's Square in Rome

Opposite page: Pope Celestine V

Pope Francis and Vatican II

Francis is the first pope of the modern era not to have attended Vatican II either as a bishop or a priest. This is significant. He takes the council as a 'given', having been ordained a Jesuit in 1969 and greatly formed by the work and spirit of the Latin American Church in terms of social justice and action for the poor. Unlike Benedict XVI, Francis does not debate the finer hermeneutical points of whether Vatican II was a council of 'continuity' or 'rupture'. In fact, he says very little about Vatican II. However, his gestures regarding Vatican II are powerful. In 2014, Pope Francis nominated Archbishop Loris Capovilla (1915-2016), personal secretary of John XXIII and witness of Vatican II, as a cardinal. In that same year, John XXIII and John Paul II were canonised. In 2018, Pope Francis canonised Paul VI. By canonising the two popes of Vatican II, Francis was signalling his approval of the council's legacy as something to be lived and not simply debated endlessly.

8 December 2015 was an important date; the fiftieth anniversary of the close of Vatican II. Some were expecting a major speech from Pope Francis, perhaps reflecting on the council from a theological perspective. Instead, referring to the significance of the date, Pope Francis announced an Extraordinary Year of Mercy. Since the moment of his election, Francis has not ceased to emphasise the infinite mercy and compassion of God. He has spoken of himself as a 'sinner' and is sometimes seen in public in St Peter's Basilica going to confession himself. A jubilee year commences with the opening of the special bronze doors of St Peter's in Rome where pilgrims enter to sacramentally participate in this event of grace. However, Pope Francis emphasised not so much pilgrims 'entering' St Peter's but going 'out' from the centre as missionaries of mercy. Bishops, priests and lay faithful are called by Pope Francis to constantly go out 'to the peripheries' to be agents of God's infinite mercy and compassion. The difference is subtle; rather than calling lapsed Catholics 'back' to sacramental practice, Pope Francis insists that active Catholics are to go 'out' and make personal and pastoral contact with those estranged from the Church.

Collegiality and synodality

One of the buzz words used constantly since Vatican II is 'collegiality'. Strictly speaking, collegiality is a theological term to describe the relationship between the pope and the bishops of the world in communion with each other, and in governing the universal Church, while respecting the supreme juridical authority of the papacy. Pope Francis has also emphasised the notion of 'synodality'. He has changed the dynamic of the Synod of Bishops normally held every three years in which he asks bishops to speak boldly and freely in the course of consultation, discernment and debate. Only recently, Pope Francis appointed Sr Nathalie Becquart of France as Under-Secretary at the Synod of Bishops. This is a significant development in the history of the Synod of Bishops and mirrors the historic appointment of Rosemary Goldie to a senior position in the Roman Curia in 1967.

Synodality is a model of governance that goes back to the early Church. The Eastern tradition of patriarchs and bishops normally meet in synod. And the Anglican church mandates national and diocesan synods.

By emphasising synodality, Pope Francis reminds us that the Church is on the journey of mission and proclamation together; and hierarchy, clergy, religious and the faithful should share together in the process of consultation and decision-making. The pope is not a monarch and the Church is not a multinational organisation. There are proper powers of governance by virtue of ordination and hierarchy. However, Vatican II greatly shifted the place of the laity from being a passive collective of those who must 'pay, pray and obey'. Pope Francis practices what he preaches. Soon after his election, he announced the formation of the 'G9', a group of nine cardinals representing the universal Church to advise him on certain matters. On any given day, the pope has supreme power in the Church to issue orders, directives and make changes that must be obeyed. However, the G9 cardinals have showed how the pope wants discernment and discussion together before changes are made. This is another demonstration of how Pope Francis lives the spirit and grace of Vatican II.

Opposite page: Pope Francis greets Catholicos Karekin II, patriarch of the Armenian Apostolic Church, during a private audience in the Apostolic Palace at the Vatican, 5 April 2018.

Below: Archbishop Mark Coleridge

> "Since the moment of his election, Francis has not ceased to emphasise the infinite mercy and compassion of God."

Australian Plenary Council

In 2016, the Australian Catholic Bishops Conference announced that Archbishop Mark Coleridge of Brisbane would lead a committee to explore a plenary council for the Church in Australia. While the announcement coincided with the final report of the royal commission into institutional sexual abuse, Archbishop Coleridge mentioned that the Church in Australia (and indeed around the world) is now ministering in a whole new cultural context than was the case twenty or thirty years ago. He insisted that for the Church, 'it cannot be business as usual'. Taking the lead from Pope Francis in terms of a synodal Church listening and discerning together, he stated that a new pastoral response is required that involves all members of the Church and not just the hierarchy and clergy. But what is a national plenary and how is it different from a synod?

When Catholics in Australia hear the word 'synod', they may associate the term with Anglicans and the requirement of regular national and diocesan synods. Any Catholic diocesan bishop has the power to summon a synod for his diocese, subject to the provisions of the 1983 Code of Canon Law and the approval of the Holy See. Once decisions are confirmed, they have the force of law in that diocese. A small number of Australian dioceses have convoked synods since Vatican II such as Brisbane (2003), Broken Bay (2011), Cairns (2008) and Canberra-Goulburn (2004). Other dioceses have convoked diocesan assemblies that do not have the canonical force of law of a synod but are still vital expressions of consultation, discernment and pastoral action at the local level.

National plenaries have been a feature of the Church in Australia. In 1844, Archbishop Polding of Sydney convoked a national plenary with the bishops of Adelaide and Hobart. The purpose of this plenary was to assist the infant church in Australia to establish itself in terms of parish missions, sacramental practice, priestly training and the provision of Catholic education. In time, more formal national plenaries were held. These were in 1885, 1895 and 1905 under the leadership of Cardinal Patrick Moran of Sydney. The last national plenary was held in 1937. However, such plenary councils were essentially 'clerical' affairs that involved bishops, senior clergy, canonists and theologians. Canons on various pastoral and disciplinary matters were prepared

and approved by Rome. Local priests and parishioners were basically told to 'abide by these rules or else!'

A new historical reality

The plenary council for Australia, initially scheduled for 2020 but postponed because of Covid, is an entirely new historical reality and not confined simply to bishops, priests and canon lawyers. While the bishops are strictly the only voting members, the exercise of consultation and development of key themes and written drafts has engaged the whole Church at a national level. Parishes, religious orders, diocesan agencies, organisations and associations of the faithful, and many individuals, constitute over 200,000 individuals who have made 17,000 submissions. These submissions have been arranged according to the following key themes:

- Missionary and evangelising
- Inclusive, participatory and synodal
- Prayerful and Eucharistic
- Humble, healing and merciful
- A joyful, hope-filled and servant community
- Open to conversion, renewal and reforming.

While certain clergy have ex officio status at the two formal plenary assemblies, the exercise of listening, consultation, discernment and discussion involves the whole Church and not just the clergy and hierarchy.

In many respects the Australian plenary promotes the key theme of Vatican II of the *sensus fidelium* – 'the faithful's sense of the faith'. While bishops are the authentic guardians and teachers of the tradition (*magisterium*), Vatican II rediscovered the rich theology of the lay faithful, the grace and dignity of baptism, and the need for the Church to be more dialogic and participatory in its life and processes. One could also say that the Australian plenary is like a 'mini council' in its scope and reach.

While a national plenary is unable to change universal Catholic teaching, the six discernment themes listed above seem to touch almost every aspect of the Church's life and ministry in Australia, with a view to renewing pastoral strategies for the challenges of this rapidly changing cultural context. Pope Francis has constantly repeated this message in his major writings such as *Evangelii Gaudium, Gaudete et Exsultate* and *Fratelli Tutti*; discernment, renewal and new pastoral strategies.

Pope Francis is exercising his ministry in a global situation in a way vastly different to the experience of Vatican II in the 1960s. The Church in Australia is also conscious that it lives in a time of great cultural change when established practices and customs are no longer 'fit for purpose'. But Vatican II did open up a new pathway with pointers that can no longer be ignored. Clergy and hierarchy are called to servant-leadership, not clerical dominance. A theologically articulate laity who take their baptism seriously must have their voices respected. Women have unique gifts of leadership and ministry that need to be employed by the Church. The drop in sacramental practice across the country calls for careful discernment and renewed pastoral action and engagement. Catholic social teaching needs to shape public debate on care for the environment. Ministry to the marginalised such as refugees, and ongoing dialogue and reconciliation with our First Peoples must occur.

Vatican II found a new language and pastoral orientation for its time. Pope Francis is encouraging the Church in Australia to do the same.

Left: Indigenous Christians at Australian Catholic Youth Festival, Perth, 2019

Bibliography

Alberigo, Giuseppe. *A Brief History of Vatican II,* Orbis Books, Maryknoll, NY, 2006.

Bonnot, Bob. *Pope John XXIII: Model and Mentor for Leaders,* St Pauls, New York, 2003.

Clark, Mary, Heather O'Connor & Valerie Krips, (eds). *Perfect Charity: Women Religious Living the Spirit of Vatican II,* Morning Star Publishers, Victoria, 2015.

Crowley, Paul. *From Vatican II to Pope Francis: Charting a Catholic future,* Orbis Books, Maryknoll, NY, 2014.

Faggioli, Massimo. *John XXIII: The Medicine of Mercy,* Liturgical Press, Collegeville, Michigan, 2014.

Faggioli, Massimo. *Vatican II: The Battle for Meaning,* Paulist Press, Mahwah, New Jersey, 2012.

Massimo Faggioli & Andrea Vinci. *The Legacy of Vatican II,* Paulist Press, New York, 2015.

Flannery, Austin. *Vatican Council II: Constitutions, Decrees, Declarations,* Costello Publishing, Northport, NY, 1996.

Gaillardetz, Richard & Catherine Clifford. *Keys to the Council: Unlocking the Teaching of Vatican II',* Liturgical Press, Collegeville, Michigan, 2012.

Goldie, Rosemary. *From a Roman Window. Five Decades of the World, the Church and Laity,* HarperCollins, Melbourne, 1998.

Gooley, Anthony. *Bite-sized Vatican II: a very basic guide to the council and its four constitutions,* St Pauls Publications, Strathfield, NSW, 2014.

Hebblewaithe, P. *John XXIII: Pope of the Council,* Geoffrey Chapman, London, 1984.

Huebsch, Bill. *Vatican II in Plain English,* (3 Volumes), Thomas More Publishing, Allen, Texas, 1997.

McEnroy, Carmel. *Guests in Their Own House: The Women of Vatican II,* Crossroads Publishing, New York, 1996.

Melloni, Alberto. *Vatican II: The Complete History,* Paulist Press, Mahwah, New Jersey, 2015.

O'Collins, Gerald. *Living Vatican II: The 21st Council for the 21st Century,* Liturgical Press, Collegeville, Michigan, 2006.

O'Collins, Gerald. *The Second Vatican Council: Message and Meaning,* Liturgical Press, Collegeville, Michigan, 2014.

O'Malley, John. *What Happened at Vatican II,* Harvard University Press, Cambridge, Massachusetts, 2008.

O'Malley, John. *When Bishops Meet: An Essay Comparing Trent, Vatican I, and Vatican II,* Harvard University Press, Cambridge, Massachusetts, 2019.

Neil Ormerod (ed). *Vatican II: Reception and implementation in the Australian Church,* Garratt Publishing, Mulgrave, Victoria, 2012.

Pilcher, Carmel (ed). *Vatican Council II: Reforming Liturgy,* ATF Theology, Adelaide, 2013.

Roncalli, Angelo. *Journal of a Soul,* Geoffrey Chapman, London, 1964.

Rush, Orm. *The Vision of Vatican II: Its Fundamental Principles,* Liturgical Press, Collegeville, Michigan, 2019.

Sullivan, Maureen. *The Road to Vatican II,* Paulist Press, Mahwah, New Jersey, 2007.

Wicks, Jared. *Investigating Vatican II: Its Theologians, Ecumenical Turn and Biblical Commitment,* Catholic University of America Press, Washington DC, 2018.

Wicks, Jared. *Doing Theology,* Paulist Press, Mahwah, New Jersey, 2009.

Zanchi, Goffredo. *John XXIII: The Official Biography,* Pauline Books & Media, Boston Massachusetts, 2001.

> "Vatican II rediscovered the rich theology of the lay faithful, the grace and dignity of baptism, and the need for the Church to be more dialogic and participatory in its life and processes."

Published in Australia by
Garratt Publishing
32 Glenvale Crescent
Mulgrave, Vic. 3170

www.garrattpublishing.com.au

Design by Lynne Muir
Text editing by Greg Hill
Cover Image: iStock

Images: Alamy pp 3, 5, 6, 14, 15, 20, 49, 51, 52
iStock pp 4, 10, 12, 28, 29, 33, 39, 41, 44, 56 Our Lady of Good Counsel and All Hallows Parish, Deepdene and Balwyn
pp 31, 36, 37, 38, 40, 42 © Chris Kapa
Wikipedia pp 1, 46, 50, 53
Diocese of Parramatta p54 ©Mary Brazell

9781922484093

Cataloguing in Publication information for this title is available from the National Library of Australia.
www.nla.gov.au

The author and publisher gratefully acknowledge the permission granted to reproduce the copyright material in this book. Every effort has been made to trace copyright holders and to obtain their permission for the use of copyright material. The publisher apologises for any errors or omissions in the above list and would be grateful if notified of any corrections that should be incorporated in future reprints or editions of this book.

Nihil Obstat: Rev Dr Cameron Forbes STD, Diocesan Censor
Imprimatur: Most Rev Peter A Comensoli DD STL Mlitt PhD Archbishop of Melbourne
Date: 12 April 2021

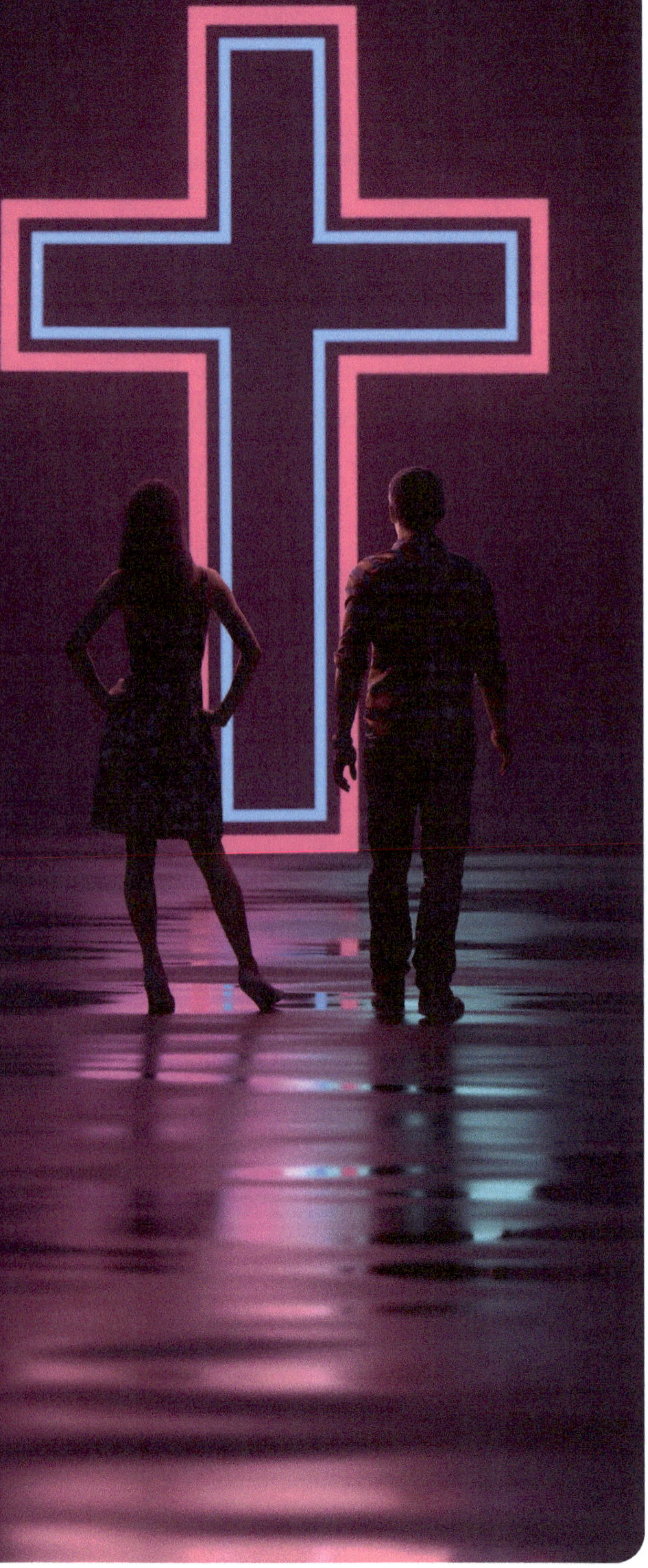

www.ingramcontent.com/pod-product-compliance
Lightning Source LLC
LaVergne TN
LVHW070408110826
845147LV00016B/972

* 9 7 8 1 9 2 2 4 8 4 0 9 3 *